Learn Resource Therapy

Clinical Qualification
Student Training Manual

Gordon Emmerson, PhD

Copyright Gordon Emmerson 2015
Old Golden Point Press
Blackwood, Victoria: Australia

ISBN-10: 0992499534

ISBN: 978-0-9924995-3-2

The purpose of Resource Therapy
is to diagnose and bring Pathological
States to Normality

Resource Therapy

Resource Therapy entails a complete theory of personality and it has interventions for a wide range of psychological presentations, from performance issues to personality disorders.

This Manual aligns with the 10 day training for a Resource Therapy International (RTI) Clinical Qualification. It is set out to ensure that all core concepts are able to be understood.

The Purpose of this manual is to enhance learning and skills either during the 10 day RT training with an official RT Trainer, or to be used as a self-training guide to learn RT skills with self-study.

Given a demonstrated proficiency gained from studying this manual, RT Trainers may grant **Recognition of Prior Learning** for parts of the ten day Clinical Qualification Training. (See page 213)

Upon the completion of training with a RT Trainer who is registered with Resource Therapy International an official RTI qualification can be gained.

www.ResourceTherapyInternational.com

Introduction

Resource Therapy Overview

The Resource Therapist first identifies the pathological condition of a state then applies the treatment actions appropriate to the condition.

Table 1 There are eight pathological conditions

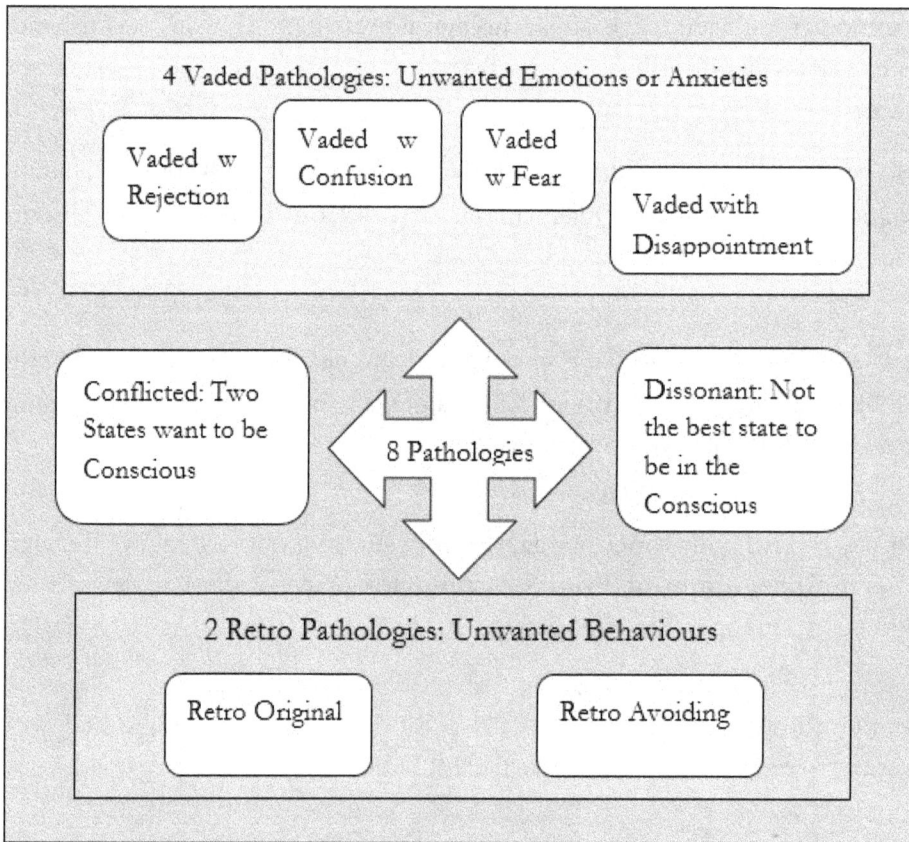

4 Vaded Pathologies: Unwanted Emotions or Anxieties

Vaded w Rejection

Vaded w Confusion

Vaded w Fear

Vaded with Disappointment

Conflicted: Two States want to be Conscious

8 Pathologies

Dissonant: Not the best state to be in the Conscious

2 Retro Pathologies: Unwanted Behaviours

Retro Original

Retro Avoiding

Table 2 The 15 Resource Therapy Treatment Actions.

RT Actions are procedures that are applied in the appropriate sequence for each of the 8 pathologies.	
1. Diagnosis of Resource Pathology	Determines which of the 8 pathologies are evident.
2. Vivify Specific	Brings the pathological resource to the conscious.
3. Bridging	Bridges from a State Vaded with Fear or Rejection to the Initial Sensitizing Event (ISE)
4. Expression	The Vaded State expresses to the Introject after bridging
5. Introject Speak	The rejecting Introject is given a voice for understanding
6. Removal	The Vaded state decides if it wants the Introject to stay
7. Relief	A helper state helps the Vaded State feel supported
8. Find Resource	The most appropriate Resource is found
9. Changing Chairs Introject Action	A state gains clarity by speaking with an Introject
10. Retro State Negotiation	Maintains the state's purpose and gives it a new role
11. Conflicted State Negotiation	Helps states respect and communicate together
12. Imagery Check	Revivifies the image in Action 2 to check progress
Complimentary Resource Actions	These are non-core useful actions

RT Actions are procedures that are applied in the appropriate sequence for each of the 8 pathologies.	
13. Resistance Alliancing	Includes a resistant state in the therapeutic process
14. The Separation Sieve	Useful metaphor tool for letting go
15. Anchoring	Assists the client to bring out the most preferred state

Table 3 Diagnosis Flowchart

What is the presenting Concern	When Conscious the State feels	Pathological Classification	Treatment Actions
Unwanted Emotions or Anxieties (Vaded States)	Fear	Vaded with Fear	2-4, 6-8, 12
	Not good enough, unlovable, or over-competitive	Vaded with Rejection	2-8, 12
	Low Energy and blocks other states from enjoyment	Vaded with Disappointment	8, 8, 10
	The state Vaded with Confusion can't stop Ruminating	Vaded with Confusion	2, 9, 12
Unwanted Behavior (Retro States)	When Conscious, Retro States feel very competent and powerful. Retro states have control and block other states out of the Conscious.	Retro Original	2, 10, 8, 12
		Retro Avoiding	2-7, 10, 12
Poor Performance	Feels incompetent	Dissonant	2, 8, 12
Internal Conflict	In conflict with another state	Conflicted	2, 11,12

The Layout of this Manual

This Manual is arranged into training days. Each training day will include:

- **Core Concepts:** Each Chapter will start with the important core concepts to be learned from that day's training.
- **Skills for each Day:** This training is about becoming a better therapist. The skills section of this manual is very important.
- **Quiz and Exercises:** At the end of each day's lesson is a short 10 question quiz to help you determine your understanding of the most important concepts.

While the answers to the quizzes are in Appendix 1, you should make a good attempt to answer all the questions before checking the answers.

This manual contains several excerpts from the books Resource Therapy Primer (2014) and Resource Therapy (2014). While those books each contain significant material that goes beyond this ten day training, the reader should be aware that parts of this training manual come directly from those texts. The larger Resource Therapy book will be an excellent reference for readers who want more detail and case examples.

Note: There are concepts that are key to being able to move pathological states to a normal condition. In this manual you will see a Star with the work Key in it when one of these concepts is covered.

Contents

1   Day 1 Resource Therapy Overview 19

1.1 Core Concepts for Day 1 Training..19

    1.1.1   The Goal of Resource Therapy 21

    1.1.2   Resource States 22

    1.1.3   Conscious 23

    1.1.4   Introjects 23

    1.1.5   Surface States 25

    1.1.6   Underlying States.. 25

    1.1.7   History 26

    1.1.8   Alters.. 28

    1.1.9   Nature of States 29

    1.1.10   Formation 30

    1.1.11   Normal States... 32

    1.1.12   Vaded 32

    1.1.13   Retro States 35

    1.1.14   Dissonant 37

    1.1.15   Conflicted States 37

    1.1.16   RT Actions 37

    1.1.17   Action 2 Vivify Specific 38

    1.1.18   Action 3 Bridging 39

1.2 Skills for Day 1..42

    1.2.1   Vivify Specific Steps.. 42

    1.2.2   Bridging Practice 42

1.3 Quiz and Activities for Day 1 Training 44

    1.3.1   Quiz.. 44

    1.3.2   Table Activities 44

1.3.3   Day 1 Crossword 47

2   Day 2 - Conflicted States 49

2.1 Core Concepts for Day 2 Training 49

2.1.1   Naming States 51

2.1.2   Action 4: Expression 51

2.1.3   Action 5 Introject Speak 52

2.1.4   Action 6 Removal 54

2.1.5   Action 7 Relief 54

2.1.6   Finding a helping State 56

2.1.7   Action 8: Find Resource 56

2.1.8   Action 11: Conflicted State Negotiation 58

2.1.9   Action 12: Imagery Check 61

2.1.10   Sensory Experience Memory 62

2.2 Skills for Day 2 65

2.2.1   Conflicted State Practice 65

2.3 Quiz and Activities for Day 2 66

2.3.1   Quiz 66

2.3.2   Table Activity 66

2.3.3   Day 2 Crossword 68

3   Day 3 RT Diagnosis & Dissonant States 71

3.1 Core Concepts for Day 3 Training 71

3.1.1   Diagnosis: Action 1 73

3.1.2   Vaded with Fear 78

3.1.3   Vaded with Rejection 80

3.1.4   Vaded with Confusion 82

3.1.6   Vaded with Disappointment 83

3.1.8   Retro Original 84

3.1.9   Retro Avoiding 85

    3.1.10   Conflicted States 88

    3.1.12   Dissonant States 90

    3.1.14   Dissonant State vs a Retro State 91

3.2 Skills for Day 3 ....**92**

    3.2.1   Resolving a Dissonant State Issue 92

3.3 Quiz and Activities for Day 3 ....**92**

    3.3.1   Quiz 92

    3.3.2   Day 3 Crossword 94

    3.3.3   Activity 95

4   Day 4 States Vaded with Confusion **97**

4.1 Core Concepts for Day 4 Training **97**

    4.1.1   Vaded with Confusion vs Disappointment 98

    4.1.2   Working with a State Vaded with Confusion 99

    4.1.3   Action 9: The Changing Chairs Introject Action 99

    4.1.4   Importance of SEMs in this Action 101

    4.1.5   Loss and Grief 102

    4.1.6   Heavy Emotions 104

4.2 Skills for Day 4 ....**105**

    4.2.1   Action 9 Changing Chairs Introject Action 105

4.3 Quiz and Activity for Day 4 Training **106**

    4.3.1   Quiz 106

    4.3.2   Activity 106

5   Day 5 States Vaded with Fear or Rejection **109**

5.1 Core Concepts for Day 5 Training **109**

    5.1.1   Panic Disorder 110

    5.1.2   Anorexia and Bulimia 112

    5.1.3   Sexual and other Abuse 115

    5.1.4   Working with a State Vaded with Fear 117

5.1.5   Working with a State Vaded with Rejection 120

5.2 Skills for Day 5 .... **124**

5.2.1   Resolving States Vaded with Fear or Rejection 125

5.3 Quiz and Activities for Day 5 Training **125**

5.3.1   Quiz 125

5.3.2   Activity 126

6   Day 6 Retro States & Vaded with Disappointment **127**

6.1 Core Concepts for Day 6 Training **127**

6.1.1   Diagnosis of Retro States 128

6.1.2   Retro Original vs Retro Avoiding 130

6.1.3   Retro State Negotiation 130

6.1.4   Addictions 132

6.1.5   Anger/Rage issues 136

6.1.6   Working with Depression 139

6.1.7   Vaded with Disappointment 141

6.1.8   Keeping purpose and trading purviews 144

6.2 Skills for Day 6 .... **145**

6.2.1   Retro State Negotiation 145

6.3 Quiz and Activities for Day 6 Training **145**

6.3.1   Quiz 145

6.3.2   Activity 146

7   Day 7 RT Mapping & Ethics **147**

7.1 Core Concepts for Day 7 Training **147**

7.1.1   Ethics: Confidentiality 148

7.1.2   Ethics: Duel Relationships 149

7.1.3   Active Listening 150

7.1.4   Resource Mapping 150

7.1.9   RT Couples Counselling 159

7.2 Skills for Day 7 ....**160**

    7.2.1   Resource Mapping 160

7.3 Quiz and Activities for Day 7 Training **161**

    7.3.1   Quiz... 161

    7.3.2   Activity 162

8   Day 8 Pain & Somatic Presentations **163**

8.1 Core Concepts for Day 8 Training....................**163**

    8.1.1   Pain and Somatic Symptoms................................ 164

    8.1.2   Organic Symptoms 165

    8.1.3   Psychosomatic Symptoms 165

    8.1.4   How to tell?.. 165

    8.1.5   Organic Intervention 167

    8.1.6   Psychosomatic Intervention 168

    8.1.7   Action 13: Resistance Alliancing......................... 169

    8.1.8   Acknowledgement, Appreciation and Suggestion 169

    8.1.9   Engagement Method 170

8.2 Skills for Day 8...**171**

    8.2.1   Practice: Pain or Somatic Symptoms................... 171

8.3 Quiz and Activities for Day 8 Training **172**

    8.3.1   Quiz... 172

    8.3.2   Activity Question 172

9   Day 9 The Separation Sieve & What Lies Within? **175**

9.1 Core Concepts for Day 9 Training....................**175**

    9.1.1   What lies within?.. 176

    9.1.2   Resource State.. 177

    9.1.3   Introject... 178

    9.1.4   Inner Self... 181

    9.1.5   Creative Form Identity (CFI) 182

9.1.6   Other Personalized Introject (OPI)..................185

9.1.7   Action 14 The Separation Sieve..........................188

9.1.8   OPI Intervention...191

9.2 Skills for Day 9 .... **193**

9.2.1   Practice: Using the Separation Sieve.................193

9.3 Quiz and Activities for Day 9 .... **194**

9.3.1   Quiz...194

9.3.2   Activity..194

10   Day 10 Review and Anchoring................................ **197**

10.1   Core Concepts for Day 10 Training....................... **197**

10.1.1   Vaded with Fear..199

10.1.2   Vaded with Rejection......................................199

10.1.3   Vaded with Confusion....................................199

10.1.4   Vaded with Disappointment............................200

10.1.5   Retro Original...200

10.1.6   Retro Avoiding..200

10.1.7   Conflicted...201

10.1.8   Dissonant...201

10.1.9   Action 15 Anchoring......................................201

10.1.10 Common Supervision Topics.........................203

10.2   Skills for Day 10 .... **209**

10.2.1   Practice: Dissonant States using Anchors.............209

10.3   Quiz and Activities for Day 10 Training **209**

10.3.1   Quiz...209

10.3.2   Day 10 Crossword..211

Recognition of Prior Learning (RPL) **213**

11   Appendix 1 Daily Activity Answers **215**

11.1   Day 1 Answers **215**

11.2   Day 2 Answers 218

11.3   Day 3 Answers 221

11.4   Day 4 Answers 224

11.5   Day 5 Answers 227

11.6   Day 6 Answers 229

11.7   Day 7 Answers 232

11.8   Day 8 Answers 234

11.9   Day 9 Answers 236

11.10   Day 10 Answers 239

12   Appendix 2 Core Concepts by Day 243

13   Glossary 251

14   Bibliography 257

Locations for the 8 Diagnoses and 15 Actions

Diagnoses

1.	Vaded with Fear -	page # 78
2.	Vaded with Rejection -	page # 80
3.	Vaded with Disappointment -	page # 83
4.	Vaded with Confusion -	page # 82
5.	Retro Original -	page # 84
6.	Retro Avoiding -	page # 85
7.	Dissonant -	page # 90
8.	Conflicted -	page # 88

Actions

1. Diagnosis of Pathology -	page # 73
2. Vivify Specific -	page # 38
3. Bridging -	page # 39
4. Expression -	page # 51
5. Introject Speak -	page # 52
6. Removal -	page # 54
7. Relief -	page # 54
8. Find Resource -	page # 56
9. Changing Chairs Introject Action-	page# 99
10. Retro State Negotiation -	page# 130
11. Conflicted State Negotiation -	page # 58
12. Imagery Check -	page # 61
Complimentary Resource Actions	
13. Resistance Alliancing -	page# 169
14. The Separation Sieve -	page# 188
15. Anchoring -	page# 201

1 Day 1 Resource Therapy Overview

Welcome to Day 1 of your Resource Therapy Training. Whether you are working through this training manual on your own or with an RTI registered trainer, you will find that reading it in the chronological order presented from day 1 to day 10 will make learning Resource Therapy easier. Each section forms an important building block which will assist your understanding and skill development in Resource Therapy.

During the first day of training there is an overview of the entire therapy, with an emphasis placed on working with Conflicted States (Action 11) and on learning the basics of Bridging from an emotional state back to childhood (Action 2). This first practice in Bridging is one where you learn to Bridge to a 'happy' time. This way you can practice Bridging before you have acquired the skills to resolve trauma. There are more terms to learn on Day 1 than on any other day of training.

Short definitions of the day one terms are provided below. It is important that you are comfortable with the fuller meaning of these terms by the end of this day's training before you continue on to Day 2.

1.1 Core Concepts for Day 1 Training

Page #'s are Hyperlinks on eBooks.		Page
Goal of RT	To move Pathological States to a Normal Condition	21
Resource States	A personality part that was created by the repetition of returning over and over again to a coping skill.	22

1.1   Core Concepts for Day 1 Training

Conscious	The awareness of self. The Conscious is held by the Resource State that is currently experiencing, aware, and behaving.	23
Introjects	A Resource State's internalized impression of another person, an animal, or an inanimate.	23
Surface States	Resources that are used frequently.	25
Underlying States	Underlying Resources are those that have been Conscious frequently in the past but currently seldom come into the Conscious.	25
History	Ferdern, Weiss, Watkins, Emmerson	26
Alters	Alters are the personality parts for those who suffer from Multiple Personality or Dissociative Identity Disorder (DID).	28
Nature of States	Because all of our Resource States have been conscious, a Resource State can be thought of as having the same personality traits as a person.	29
Formation	Resources are personality parts that first developed as coping mechanisms for the client.	30
Normal States	Resources in the Normal condition exhibit psychological health.	32
Vaded	States that have Emotions that interfere with the client's life.	32
Retro	States that do Behaviors that interfere with the client's life.	35
Dissonant	States that are in the Conscious at the wrong time.	37

1.1 Core Concepts for Day 1 Training

Conflicted	States that don't understand and respect each other. They fight.	37
Actions	Structured Techniques of Resource Therapy	37
Action 2 Vivify Specific	The Action that brings the wanted Resource State to the Conscious.	38
Action 3 Bridging	The Action that moves from an unwanted emotion to the ISE.	39

1.1.1 The Goal of Resource Therapy

Resource Therapy works by insuring that the therapist works directly with the state that needs change. Often a client will go to therapy and tell about a problem. The client begins talking with the therapist in a state that does not like another state. When the therapist continues to talk with this state that does not like another state, there is little power for change. The real power for change is when the therapist brings into the Conscious the pathological state and works directly with it.

The goal of resource therapy is for pathological states to return to a state of normality. This is accomplished via a 4 step process of 1) Aim: Determine what the client is ready to change, 2) Classify: Diagnose the pathological state as one of the eight pathological categories, 3) Actions: Intervene with the appropriate Actions for the diagnosis, and 4) Review: Debrief with the client.

Table 4: The Resource Therapy Process (ACAR)

RT Process	
Aim	Determine what the client is ready to change.
Classify	Diagnose the Pathological Resource State into a category.
Actions	Follow the prescribed RT Actions for the Classification.
Review	Debrief with the client.

Resource Therapists learn the 15 RT Treatment Actions, or therapeutic techniques. Prescribed combinations of these are used to move pathological Resource States to normality.

1.1.2   Resource States

Our Resource States are the different parts of our personality. We each have many Resources and just like the states of a country can go together to make up the country, Resources go together to make up the personality. One resource can be pathological while others can be normal.

Key
Resource: A personality part that was created by the repetition of returning over and over again to a coping skill. It is a physiological part of the nervous system created by axon and dendrite growth and trained synaptic firings. Each Resource manifests the traits of the coping skill that formed it. Each will have its own level of emotion, intellect, and abilities. Whenever a person is Conscious there is a Resource State holding the Conscious.

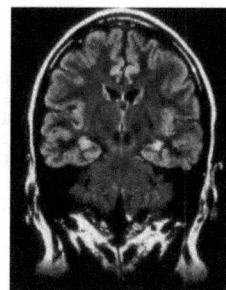

When a Resource is 'Conscious' it is out and it has control of the personality. For example, when a person is currently in a joking, light hearted mood, that Resource State is referred to as the 'Conscious' state. Other personality parts that may be fragile, reactive, intellectual, or reflective do not at that time hold the Conscious.

A person will not experience the symptoms of a pathology unless a state related to that pathology is 'Conscious'. The 'subconscious' is the collection of Underlying Resource States that are not currently conscious or observing.

A Resource is a physiological part of the brain, a neural pathway that has been made over time. Each Resource is different from the others with different traits.

1.1.3 Conscious

Conscious: The awareness of self. The Conscious is held by the Resource State that is currently experiencing, aware, and behaving. When a different Resource State takes over the Conscious, sense of self, emotions, behavior and abilities change. What the person experiences, the Conscious awareness, may change from intellectual and reflective, to reactive and emotional with a change of Resource State.

Key

The client suffering from OCD, while doing checking behavior, will have a Resource in the Conscious as he or she feels and thinks, "I have to check these locks," but when another Resource becomes Conscious the client will likely detest that checking Resource and wish it was not there. Those two Resources are conflicted. A person who says, "I hate myself when I am like that," is expressing from one Resource about another Resource. In Resource Personality Theory the terms Resource and Resource State are synonymous.

1.1.4 Introjects

Introjects are our internalized impressions of another person, an animal, or even an inanimate, like a flood, a fire, a storm, or a fictional character.

We will have an Introject, an internalized impression, of every person we know. Most are pleasant and loving, although some are not. It is **Introjects** that

Vaded States internally fear, feel rejected by, feel disappointed by, or feel

confusion about. Introjects have no power of their own although states can hold the illusion that Introjects have power. They only have the power that a Resource State grants them within the internalized impression that it holds of them. Real people may have power. Introjects do not. The person that an Introject represents may be real, but an Introject is merely a memory fragment. Resource Therapy techniques makes it clear to the client's states that they, themselves, hold the real power and feared Introjects can be internally shrunk and cleared.

While a Resource is a physiological part of the brain that has developed with axon and dendrite growth during the repetition of a useful coping skill, an Introject is merely an impression that a Resource holds. It is interesting that an Introject may be feared by a Resource State.

A state is helped with the understanding that the Introject it has feared, felt rejected by, been disappointed by, or felt confusion about is not real. It may be appropriate for the client to fear a real person, but there is no utility in fearing an Introject, a memory fragment.

Introject: A Resource State's internalized impression of another person, an animal, or an inanimate. Most Introjects are experienced as emotionally positive, but Vaded States hold Introjects from which they have experienced negative emotion. These Introjects have only the power given them by the Resource States that hold them.

Key

Introjects are Resource State specific. That means that one Resource may hold an Introject of the person, John, and another Resource may hold a different Introject (impression) of the same person. One Resource may see John as an important friend, while another Resource may distrust, or dislike John. A battered client may have a Resource that hates their battering partner, Terry, but when another Resource is Conscious that same client may feel a love and need for Terry.

This state dependent Introjection is most evident with people suffering from DID, multiple personality disorder. One alter may know an individual well, while another alter may not know the same person at all.

The fact that Resources have their own **Introjects** means that one Resource may hold an unfulfilled need to gain love from a parent, while another Resource may either know it has that love from that parent, or may not be interested in having that love at all. A Vaded childhood Resource may fear an older, bigger cousin, while the adult Resource may hold no fear of that person.

The understanding that clients have a number of Resources, each holding their own Introjects, is very important when working in therapy, because clients often respond to the therapist from a mature, intellectual, talkative Resource State. This intellectual Resource State will have different feelings about, for example, a parent, than will other underlying Resources that may have been vaded by that parent. The most powerful therapeutic interventions work directly with the Resource States that are pathological.

1.1.5   Surface States

Surface Resources, as opposed to Underlying Resources, are those that are used frequently. They normally share memories together, and often observe other Surface States when one is in the Conscious. A Resource that is out at work, and a Resource that is out while travelling are examples of Surface States.

If you think of a classroom, the students on the front row could represent the Surface States. They are present and do most of the talking. The students further back are Underlying States. A student in the back of the room may be upset and that can disturb the whole class (the personality). It would do little good to talk with a student sitting in the front row to help the upset student in the back. That is what some therapies attempt; to talk only with an intellectual state hoping to solve the issue of another state.

1.1.6   Underlying States

Underlying Resources, as opposed to Surface Resources, are those that have been Conscious frequently in the past but currently seldom come into the Conscious. Most childhood states are Underlying Resources, with memories not readily available to Surface States. Vaded (upset) States

are most commonly Underlying States, which occasionally come to the Conscious holding their upset feelings.

1.1.7   History

Austrian, Paul Federn (1871-1950), a contemporary of Freud, first defined the personality as composed of parts. He saw distinct states that individuals moved into and out of, and noted that as they do, no matter which state individuals operated from their ego was present. Federn called these personality parts Ego States (Federn, 1953).

These personality parts are termed Resources in Resource Personality Theory. Federn's, and later Italian, Edoardo Weiss' (1889-1970) conception of the personality (1950) was re-interpreted by American, John (1913-2012) and German born, Helen (1921-2002) Watkins (1997), in their conception of Ego State Therapy, and by Australian, Gordon Emmerson (1950-present) in his conception of Resource Therapy (2014).

Differences between Resource Therapy and Ego State therapy

1. Hypnosis: Resource Therapists hold that the use of the treatment Actions provide a sufficient level of focus for therapeutic change, while Ego State Therapists use hypnotic inductions.

2. Introjects: Resource Therapists see Introjects as internalized impressions empowered only by the Resource States that hold them, while Ego State Therapists see them as Ego States (this difference is key in the treatment).

3. States holding trauma: Resource Therapists believe internal protagonists are powerless memory fragments and to fight them is to empower them. Resource Therapists help the client to gain an understanding that they

have no internal power. Ego State Therapists help clients fight internal protagonists.

4. Diagnostic Criteria: Resource Therapy has diagnostic criteria for 8 pathological conditions, and 15 corresponding Treatment Actions. Ego State Therapy does not have distinct diagnostic criteria for state conditions.

5. The Nature of the States: Resource Therapists believe personality parts are Resources that developed as coping skills and therefore each is a tool that can be useful, while the Watkins saw personality parts developing from the personality splitting; "split off from the core ego because of trauma" (Watkins & Watkins, 1997, pp. 26).

Emmerson's contributions to Resource Therapy are summarized below

Table 5: Theoretical and Technique Developments for Resource Therapy			
Personality Theory based on Personality Parts being physiological neural growth, formed by the repetition of coping skills.			2006
The Concept of Surface and Underlying States, and State Specific Introjects			2003
State Conditions: Normal, Retro, Vaded, Conflicted (coined the term Vaded)			2006
Other aspects of state conditions	Vaded with Fear Vaded with Rejection Vaded with Confusion Vaded with Disappointment	Vaded Conscious Vaded Avoided Retro Original Retro Avoiding Dissonant States	2013
Criteria for Diagnosis into state condition pathological category, and the concept of Sensory Experience Memory			2014
Therapy Process: ACAR – Aim, Classify, Actions, Review			2014

Table 5: Theoretical and Technique Developments for Resource Therapy			
Specific intervention techniques including: Depression, OCD, Addictions, Couples Counselling, Eating Disorders, Crisis Intervention, Grief, DID, Rage, Anti-Social Behavior			2002-2014
Bridging process of Vivify Specific, Attain Age, Funnel			2006
Designated 15 Detailed Therapeutic Actions, including:	Vivify Specific Expression, Introject Speak Removal, Relief Retro State Negotiation	Find Resource Resistance Alliancing Separation Sieve Conflicted State Negotiation	2004-2014

1.1.8   Alters

Alters are the personality parts for those who suffer from Multiple Personality or DID. The personality is made up of parts that are called Resource States.

These Resource States are something that everyone has.   During early childhood, during severe and chronic abuse, some children will develop the coping skill of 'not thinking about the abuse' the next day, while in a different state. With practice some children can get very good at this, 'not thinking about the abuse'. The communication links between their states atrophies over time, so when in one state, that state has no memory of what happened while they were in a different state. It proves to be a useful coping skill, but results in the personality parts not being able to share memories, and at this point the personality states become alters. Alters do not share memories with each other. The current term for this is DID (Dissociative Identity Disorder), but it is more popularly known as Multiple Personality.

Surface States in the normal personality that have not thought about early childhood memories for a long time will most often not be able to remember early childhood very well, for the same reason. Those memories have not been revisited for so long the synaptic connections between the states has atrophied. When childhood states are brought into the conscious they bring with them their memories of childhood.

Working with DID is covered in the Advanced Clinical Training. It is a process of gaining trust from alters, having alters practice talking directly with each other in therapy (at first they will not remember what was said by the other alter) and bridging to, and working with, trauma.

1.1.9   Nature of States

Whenever we are conscious we are in a Resource State. Because all of our Resource States have at some point been conscious, a Resource State can be thought of as having the same personality traits as a person. They like to be liked and they like to be respected. Our Resource states are us. We like to be spoken to with respect. Therefore, when working with a client it is important to talk to, and about, Resource States with respect.

If a state hears you talking about it with disrespect it will not be as cooperative as it will when you talk about it as important and useful. For example, if a client presents with an issue of procrastination there is a state that wants to get more work done, and another state that wants to rest or play. When speaking with the state that wants to get more work done it is good to show understanding for its wishes, but also to show understanding for the value of rest or play. Then, if you are talking with the tired state that needs to rest the body it will feel like you are an ally that is understanding.

Resource States also like to be spoken with directly. It is good to call a resource state by name, and speak with it directly in a tone that fits its personality. For example, if you are talking to a rest state that has named itself Rest, it might be good to say something like, "Rest, you sound like a very important part of this person to make sure the body is recharged and ready for other states to use." When a state feels directly spoken to, and respected, it stays in the conscious and is more cooperative.

1.1.10 Formation

Resources are personality parts that first developed as coping mechanisms for the client. When a coping skill was developed, especially early in life, and returned to over and over again, the repetitive behavior caused specific axon and dendrite growth, and trained synaptic connections. This repetitive training creates a personality part that can be returned to when its function is needed.

The formulation of the personality and the formulation of the Resources coincide. Most Resources develop during childhood and early adolescence, although it is possible for new Resources to develop in adulthood, given sufficient training. Resource development is a physiological development.

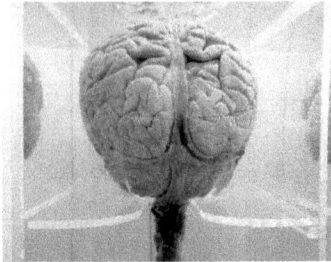

Animal studies have made it clear that the brain develops according to stimulation. Animals that have been exposed to enhanced activity had enhanced brain growth. Their brains grow more and weigh more. Axon and dendrite growth and the development of synaptic connections vary, both according to the amount of stimulation and inrelation to the type of stimulation. Schrott (1997) overviewed a number of studies, both animal and human that indicate the brain develops 'profoundly' in relation to the stimulation it receives.

Muir, Dalhousie, and Mitchell (1975) demonstrated how the brains of kittens develop in early life in relation to vision. During the first four months of life the vision of kittens was confined to contours of a single orientation (using special lenses), either vertical or horizontal. Kittens that were raised where they could only view a vertical orientation of their surroundings during their first four months were later less able to see horizontal shapes, and kittens that were raised where they could only view a horizontal orientation of their surroundings during their first four months were later less able to see vertical shapes. Numerous other animal studies confirm that the brain develops according to the particular type of stimulation it receives (Levin, 2010; Wilkinson & Frances, 1995; Blakemore, 1987; Wark, Peck, & Carol, 1982; Buisseret, Gary-Bobo, & Imbery, 1982). This indicates that the brain grows according to the exact stimulation it receives. This is how we grow our personal set of Resource States, by growing them with the stimulation they get while we practice our coping skills.

Not only do brains grow according to stimulation, but existing synapses fire more easily with repetitive practice. The first time something is attempted, whether it is a physical activity or mental learning task, ability is normally low, but with repetition the same activity or task may become easy and commonplace (Brych & Fisher, 2011).

Resource Personality Theory is based on the evidence that the brain is formed, and is trained through repetition. During early childhood, if the child is nurturing to a parent and receives positive feedback for this nurturing behavior, the child may return over and over again to this nurturing behavior to receive the positive feedback. This repetition of nurturance can create a nurturing Resource; that is, a neural pathway made by axon and dendrite connections and trained synaptic firing that may be activated in the future when the person wants positive feedback. Physiological brain growth and training from repeated practice creates this neural pathway, this Resource. When this Resource comes into the Conscious it brings with it its particular level of feelings, intellect and the skills it has learned during the repetitive behavior that formed it.

For example, a child who wanted attention (unmet need) might attempt to gain that attention by telling a joke or by doing something funny (coping skill). If that child got the wanted attention from this behavior and returned repeatedly to that behavior over and over again that child would develop a joking Resource. Later in life, when that child needs attention, he or she may tell a joke or do something funny, because the joking Resource is activated.

A different child, who found attempts at being funny unsuccessful, would not develop a joking Resource. Therefore, each individual has his or her own Resource map. This Resource map is what defines personality (Emmerson, 2011). Each person has a number of Resources, and those Resources will be in one of the five conditions, Normal, Conflicted, Vaded, Dissonant, or Retro (Emmerson, 2006).

If the child learns, in a family where there is a lot of yelling and screaming, that withdrawing and being quiet results in 'Keeping out of trouble', and if this withdrawing occurs repetitively to the benefit of the child then a withdrawing Resource may develop. In childhood, and later in life, when this person is confronted with anger or loudness, this withdrawing Resource may emerge, giving the person the feelings of being frightened and having to be quiet. When a client feels inner conflict in relation to this behavior the withdrawing Resource becomes a Retro Original State, a Resource whose behavior is not wanted by other states.

Resource States are physiological. They are a result of normal brain development. They are a result of axon and dendrite development and of synaptic training. They become a part of the personality. Each person has an undetermined number of Resource State neural pathways, numbering at least in double digits. Resources can be divided roughly into two types, Surface (used often) and Underlying (rarely used), and the state a person is experiencing life from at any time is called the Conscious state.

1.1.11   Normal States

Resources in the Normal condition exhibit psychological health. They function well externally and within the personality. They are not conflicted with other states and they do not hold psychological distress. It is the purpose of Resource Therapy for all states to achieve a normal condition.

1.1.12   Vaded

Vaded States are Resource States that have become overwhelmed by negative emotion to the point where they can no longer carry out their normal functions, and when they come to the Conscious they bring their negative emotions with them, resulting in the client feeling upset and out-of-control.

When a Vaded State becomes conscious the client feels bad emotionally, and this can be experienced as anxiety, fear, frustration, panic, or even an undefined negative feeling. There is most often an Initial Sensitizing Event that relates to when a Normal State became Vaded, and helping the Vaded State reframe the Introjects it holds around this event can return it to a state of normality. Vaded States are the origin of a number of psychological issues that will be detailed in this training.

All Vaded States have in common the fact that they were Normal functioning Resources that were developed to fulfill a function prior to the time they became Vaded. Once Vaded, these states are no longer able to fulfill their normal function, until they become resolved.

Traumatic incidents do not always vade Resources. Following a traumatic incident, if the individual gets support and understanding, is able to talk about what happened, and is able to gain some perspective then the Resource will not be Vaded. This underlines the importance of crisis intervention therapy. It is often family or friends who are able to offer understanding and support.

Most Resources that become Vaded are vaded in childhood. Children often feel unable to ask for help or support, and may not have the experience to do so. Sometimes they feel they would get into trouble if they tried to talk to someone about their issues. A state is Vaded when it experiences something outside of its ability to deal with emotionally, and it does not gain a resolution.

Table 6: Stage of Development when Normal states become Vaded

	Vaded with Fear	Vaded with Rejection	Vaded with Confusion	Vaded with Disappointment
Childhood	Predominately	Predominately	Occasionally	Occasionally
Adulthood	Occasionally	Occasionally	Predominately	Predominately

Adults may also have experiences outside their ability to cope, and when this happens without proper crisis intervention they too may experience the vading of a Resource. Adult onset PTSD is an example of this. PTSD is the result of a Resource that has experienced a life-threatening situation and has not received proper emotional resolution.

Resources may be Vaded in four ways. They may be

- **Vaded with Fear**: (Phobias, PTSD, Panic, situational fear),
- **Vaded with Rejection**: (Feeling worthless or unlovable, high need for approval),
- **Vaded with Confusion**: (Rumination, confusion), or
- **Vaded with Disappointment**: (Depression, Despair).

Each of these types of Vaded States may result in an array of psychological disturbance. The following sections will detail the types of disturbance that can be attributed to each type of Vaded State.

Vaded States cause psychological issues in two ways:

- **Vaded Conscious:** These states come into the Conscious giving the client the negative feelings they hold, along with a feeling of being out of control. This state may feel emotionality, anxiety, or have feelings of worthlessness, confusion or despair. Examples include, PTSD, Depression, Panic Disorders, Anxiety, Phobias and others. States Vaded with Disappointment or Confusion will manifest as Vaded Conscious States, while states Vaded with Fear or Rejection may manifest as Vaded Conscious States or they may be avoided by Retro State Avoiding behavior.

- **Vaded Avoided States:** These Vaded Avoided States come into or near the surface then are driven from the surface by avoidance behavior. It is the behavior of a Retro Avoiding State (described below) that directs the Vaded State away from surface consciousness in order to avoid the negative feelings of the Vaded State. Examples include, Addictions, OCD, Eating Disorders, Anti-Social Behaviors, and others. These states may be Vaded with Fear or Rejection.

Table 7: Pathological Manifestation of Vaded States

	Vaded with Fear	Vaded with Rejection	Vaded with Confusion	Vaded with Disappointment
When Vaded Conscious States	Phobias, PTSD, Panic, situational fear	Feeling worthless or unlovable, high need for approval	Rumination, confusion	Depression, Despair
When Vaded Avoided States (are driven from the Consciousness by Retro Avoiding States)	Addictions, Drug Taking, OCD, Withdrawal Anger	Eating Disorders, Work/relationship avoidance, Shopping Addiction, 'Perfectionistic' behavior	Sleeplessness, Inability to concentrate, can't let go.	Withdrawal, Anti-Depressant Medication

1.1.13   Retro States

Retro states do behavior that other states do not like. "I hate myself when I do that," or "I wish I did not do that," are examples of one state talking about a Retro State.

Retro states, when conscious, act in ways that other Resources (and usually other people) find problematic. The two types of Retro States, **Retro Original States** and **Retro Avoiding States** are described below.

- **Retro Original States** are states that have learned a functional coping skill in childhood that is no longer wanted by the client. Much antisocial behavior is a result of **Retro Original States** and examples include passive aggressive behavior and rage. These Retro States will continue to see their role as important, until they can be negotiated with to take on an altered or lesser role.

- **Retro Avoiding States** learn to hold the Consciousness to avoid the experience of a Vaded State. In problem gambling, the state that gambles is a Retro Avoiding State. It has learned to protect the client from a

painful Vaded emotion filled state by filling the Consciousness with gambling activity. Other Resources will dislike this gambling Resource, but the Retro State believes its role in saving the client from the negative emotions of the Vaded State is more important than the disapproval it endures. Other examples of Retro Avoiding States include the states that cause a client to feel numb, states that act out OCD behavior, self-harming behavior, and states that are involved with eating disorder activities and addictions. These states will hold a strong compulsion to maintain their "helping" behavior until the feelings of the Vaded State are resolved.

Table 8: Pathological Manifestations of Retro States by Type

Retro Original State Behaviors	Retro Avoiding State Behaviors	
Pouting, Anti-Social Behavior, Rage, Personality Disorders, Passive Aggressive Behavior	Addictions, Drug Taking, OCD, Withdrawal, Anger Eating Disorders, Work/relationship avoidance, Shopping Addiction, 'Perfectionistic' behavior, Self-Harming behavior.	Retro Original Behavior is learned in childhood as a coping mechanism during the development of the Resource State. Retro Avoiding Behavior is used as an escape mechanism to assist the personality to avoid the traumatic feelings of a State Vaded with Fear or Rejection.

Table 9 Stage of Development when states begin Retro Behavior

	Retro Original States	Retro Avoiding States	
Childhood	Predominately	Occasionally	Behavior becomes Retro when other States wish it would not happen. A behavior that all states view as OK is not Retro Behavior.
Adulthood	Occasionally	Predominately	

1.1.14 Dissonant

Dissonant States are Resources that would otherwise be normal, except the Dissonant State is not the preferred state to hold the Conscious. The Dissonant state is uncomfortable in the Conscious, and it would prefer another state to take over. Examples of this is having the wrong state out when testing, when playing a sport, or when dealing with a boss, a partner, or a child.

1.1.15 Conflicted States

Conflicted States are Resources in a level of conflict with another Resource to the extent that the individual experiences psychological distress.

While it is common and appropriate that Resources hold different opinions ['I would really like the car', and 'there's no way I can afford a new car'] conflicted states acquire a level of conflict that becomes stressful to the client. A 'work state' and a 'rest state' may be in conflict over the activity of the client, which is the case when a client presents with procrastination. A state that wants to sleep and a state that wants to think can be in conflict, which can result in insomnia.

1.1.16 RT Actions

It can be confusing to know exactly what to do in therapy. How do we select the right procedures? How do we move pathological states to a Normal Condition?

Resource Therapy Actions are techniques that allow Resource Therapists to move pathological states to normality. See the Introduction of this manual for a complete list of the 15 Actions. These Actions will be taught throughout the training.

Clients come to therapy because of pathological states. The first question of a Resource Therapist is, "What is it that you are ready to change today?" The way the client answers this question helps the therapist with the first Action, Diagnosis. When the therapist diagnoses a pathological state into one of the eight pathological classifications a specific set of prescribed resource Actions will help the therapist bring the troubled state into a state of normality.

1.1.17   Action 2 Vivify Specific

The Vivify Specific Action is one of the most used Actions in Resource Therapy. Resource Therapy is powerful because the Resource State that has a problem is worked with directly. The Vivify Specific Action is the Action that ensures that the right state is out for therapeutic work.

In order to bring the right state out it is **IMPERATIVE** to ensure that the client describes **ONE SPECIFIC TIME** when that state was experienced. It is incumbent upon the therapist to not accept a statement that signifies a general time that state might be out, such as, "When I am at home." The client must describe one specific incident when the state was out.

When the client is able to describe one specific incident when the state was conscious the therapist should ask the client to, "Just allow your eyes to close so you can focus on this better."

Following the closure of eyes, the therapist should begin speaking in **PRESENT TENSE** terms. For example, "With your boss in front of you right now, what kind of expression does he have on his face?" Using these types of present tense questions, a lot of detail should be gathered about what the client is experiencing within and during this incident. The following questions are examples of the kinds of details that may help ensure that the desired Resource State becomes Conscious.

- "As you are sitting there on the grass, what time of day is it?"

- "Is it sunny, or overcast? What is the temperature like?"

- "What expression are you noticing on your partner's face right now?"

- "Exactly how are you feeling, right now, as your partner has this expression?"

- "Are there other people watching you now?"

These kinds of questions may be asked until it becomes evident that the Resource State is in the Conscious. If you are attempting to bring a Vaded Resource State into the Conscious you will be able to see a level of emotion, or affect, exhibited by the client at this time.

If you are attempting to bring a Retro State into the Conscious you will notice that you are talking with a state that feels like it has an important role. If you are bringing a Conflicted State into the Conscious you will notice that it shows a level of frustration, dislike, or disapproval about another state. If you are bringing a Dissonant State into the Conscious you will notice that this state does not like being Conscious in the Vivify Specific moment. It will feel incompetent or uncomfortable. If you are bringing a Vaded State into the conscious you will notice that the client is experiencing something upsetting or anxiety provoking. The client may feel overwhelmed.

1.1.18   Action 3 Bridging

Sometimes clients will report that they know why they had the emotions they do. I find that when they say this they are often mistaken. Bridging is able to reveal exactly what is connected with the Vaded State that is Vaded with Fear or Rejection.

Bridging is important because it links the unwanted emotions of the Vaded States with Fear or Rejection to the initial sensitizing event when they were originally Vaded.

It is only by locating the original sensitizing event that the State Vaded with Fear or Rejection may be resolved.

For example, a client may not be able to speak in front of a group because he has a state that was Vaded as a child when he was yelled at by his father. That precise state is still holding a fear of his father Introject from the time it was Vaded. That state will continue to hold that fear until the initial sensitizing event is revisited and the Vaded State becomes empowered. Therefore, it is extremely important for Bridging to take the State Vaded with Fear or Rejection to the initial sensitizing event.

Bridging entails three simple steps:
1. Vivify Specific
2. Attain an age for the state.
3. Funnel the state into the initial sensitizing event.

The first step is RT Action 2, Vivify Specific. Step 2 continues immediately after Vivify Specific, while the client's eyes are still closed. The second step is to get the Vaded State that is currently in the Conscious, following step one, to express how old it feels. This can be a little tricky because often if you ask, "How old do you feel?" the client will merely report the current age. The actual Vaded State will feel the same age that it was at the time that it became Vaded, during the initial sensitizing event.

If, while the Vaded State is speaking you hear a voice that sounds like the voice of a child you can say something like, "It sounds like I'm hearing the voice of a child right now. About how old would that child be?" If this opportunity does not present itself, I often use the following sequence of questions in order to get the age that the Vaded State feels.

- "Where exactly in your body are you experiencing this feeling of...?" (mention the feeling that has already been expressed)

- "About how big an area does that cover, the size of a golf ball, a tennis ball, a football?"

- "Are the edges of that area distinct, or do they muffle out?"

- "Inside that area, is there a shade of lightness or darkness?"

- "Inside that area, is there a color?"

- "Is that color, or shade, consistent across the whole area, or is it darker in the middle?"

- "If you are standing inside that area right now, is it thick in there, or thin and easy to move?"

- "If you are just sitting on the edge of that area dangling your feet down into that (for example, thick dark red stuff), is it easy to move your feet back and forth, or difficult."

- "What do your feet feel like as you push them back and forth?"

- "Notice what your feet look like in that stuff and tell me what they look like?"

At this point clients will almost always say that their feet look smaller. When they do, asked them, "About what age would those feet be?" This series of questions will most normally provide the age of the state at the time that it was Vaded. Even if it is impossible to get an age Bridging may continue with more general questions about kinds of images that are noticed.

The third and final step of Bridging is to funnel the client into the image of the initial sensitizing event. In order to funnel the client into the image of the initial sensitizing event I usually use the following questions.

- "Being (for example, seven) right now and feeling (for example, like no matter what you say you're going to be in trouble), does it feel like you are more inside a building or outside a building?"

- "Does it feel like you are more alone, or does it feel like someone else is there?"

- (If someone else is there) "Who else is there?"

- "What is happening?"

There is no need for the client to go into detail in terms of what is happening. What is important is that clients connect with the initial sensitizing event so that they can become empowered over that event using the appropriate RT Actions.

1.2 Skills for Day 1

The skills that are to be practiced on Day 1 are Vivify Specific (Action 2) and Bridging (Action 3). It is very important to practice these, as you can only be ready for client work when you have the skills and understanding that is gained from practice. For video examples go to www.tinyurl.com/learnresourcetherapy.

Vivify Specific is one of the most used actions, as it is the action that allows the therapist to bring into the Conscious any preferred Resource State. This action is covered in some detail on page 38 in this text, and is further explained with client transcripts in Resource Therapy (2014). The steps are as follows:

1.2.1 Vivify Specific Steps

1. Find one single, specific time the desired state was in the Conscious. This cannot be a general time, such as, "Often with my wife."

2. Ask the Client to allow his or her eyes to close.

3. Begin speaking in the present tense and ask a number of questions to vivify a continuing number of aspects about being in this event, e.g., "As she is looking at you right now, what expression is on her face?"

4. Continue vivifying until you notice that the state you want to speak with is obviously in the Conscious.

5. Ask this Conscious State, "What can I call you, right now, as you are having this experience?"

1.2.2 Bridging Practice

Bridging is another important skill, and it is probably the most artful aspect of Resource Therapy. It often takes students a period of time before they feel proficient in Bridging, therefore it is important to start the practice early.

When a client has a state Vaded with Fear or Rejection it is important to Bridge to the Initial Sensitising Event (ISE) so the state Vaded with Fear can learn by experience that the Introject from that ISE no longer has any power, or for the state Vaded with Rejection to gain a feeling of unconditional love.

The practice on Day 1 will not involve therapy, which is good because the tools to move Vaded States to Normality will be covered later in the training. On Day 1 the practice is to learn to Bridge to a happy time. This is enjoyable for the client and this practice client can be a friend or family member.

Bridging Steps

1. Vivify Specific to make sure the state Vaded with Fear or Rejection is currently Conscious.

2. Continue to define the state with the feelings it has given, while getting the age this upset state feels.

    a. This can be done with the, 'It sounds like I am hearing the voice of a child. How old a child has this voice.'

    b. Or, after defining where the feeling is, e.g., in the chest or stomach, get a clear picture of that area in the body with questions such as, size, shade, color, thickness, etc., then asked the emotional state to, 'Sit on the edge of that area, dangling your feet into the middle of that stuff. Look at your feet and tell me what they look like. How old would a person with feet like that be?'

    c. Or, you can be creative to discover the age feeling of the state that feels little and out of control.

3. Funnel, using the age, the client to the ISE, with questions like:

    a. Being (for example) 5 right now, does it seem like you are more inside a building or outside?

    b. Is it more light or dark where you are having these feelings right now, being (5)?

    c. Are you alone or is there someone else there?

    d. Tell me what is happening.

    For video examples go to www.tinyurl.com/learnresourcetherapy.

1.3   Quiz and Activities for Day 1 Training

1.3.1   Quiz

1.   What is the purpose of the Vivify Specific Action?

2.   What is the purpose of Bridging?

3.   What is the difference between Surface and Underlying States?

4.   Where do Resource States come from?

5.   What are Introjects?

6.   What are pathological states called that have unwanted feelings?

7.   What are pathological states called that do unwanted behaviors?

8.   What are pathological states called that are in conflict with other states to the point of anxiety?

9.   What are states called that prefer not to be out when they are, and wish another state would take over?

10. What does it mean to talk in the present tense?

(Answers are in Appendix 1. Try to get them all right before you look.)

1.3.2   Table Activities

Fill in the Eight Pathological Conditions in the Table below.

What is the presenting Concern	When Conscious the State feels	Pathological Classification	Treatment Actions
Unwanted Emotions or Anxieties (Vaded States)	Fear		2-4, 6-8, 12
	Not good enough or unlovable		2-8, 12

What is the presenting Concern	When Conscious the State feels	Pathological Classification	Treatment Actions
	Low Energy and blocks other states from enjoyment		8, 8, 10
	The state Vaded with Confusion can't stop Ruminating		2, 9, 12
Unwanted Behavior (Retro States)	When Conscious, Retro States feel very competent and powerful. Retro states have control and block other states out of the Conscious.		2, 10, 8, 12
			2-7, 10, 12
Poor Performance	Feels incompetent		2, 8, 12
Internal Conflict	In conflict with another state		2, 11,12

See Table 3 Diagnosis Flowchart, page vii.

Fill in the 15 Actions in the Table Below.

RT Actions are therapy intervention procedures.	
1.	Determines which of the 8 pathologies are evident.
2.	Brings the pathological resource to the conscious.
3.	Bridges from a State Vaded with Fear or Rejection to ISE
4.	The Vaded State expresses to the Introject after bridging

RT Actions are therapy intervention procedures.	
5.	The rejecting Introject is given a voice for understanding
6.	The Vaded state decides if it wants the Introject to stay
7.	A helper state helps the Vaded State feel supported
8.	The most appropriate Resource is found
9.	A state gains clarity by speaking with an Introject
10.	Maintains the state's purpose gives it a new role
11.	Helps states respect and communicate together
12.	Revivifies the image in Action 2 to check progress
Complimentary Resource Actions	These are non-core useful actions
13.	Includes a resistant state in the therapeutic process
14.	Useful metaphor tool for letting go
15.	Assists the client to bring out the most preferred state

See Table 2 The 15 Resource Therapy Treatment Actions., page v.

1.3.3 Day 1 Crossword

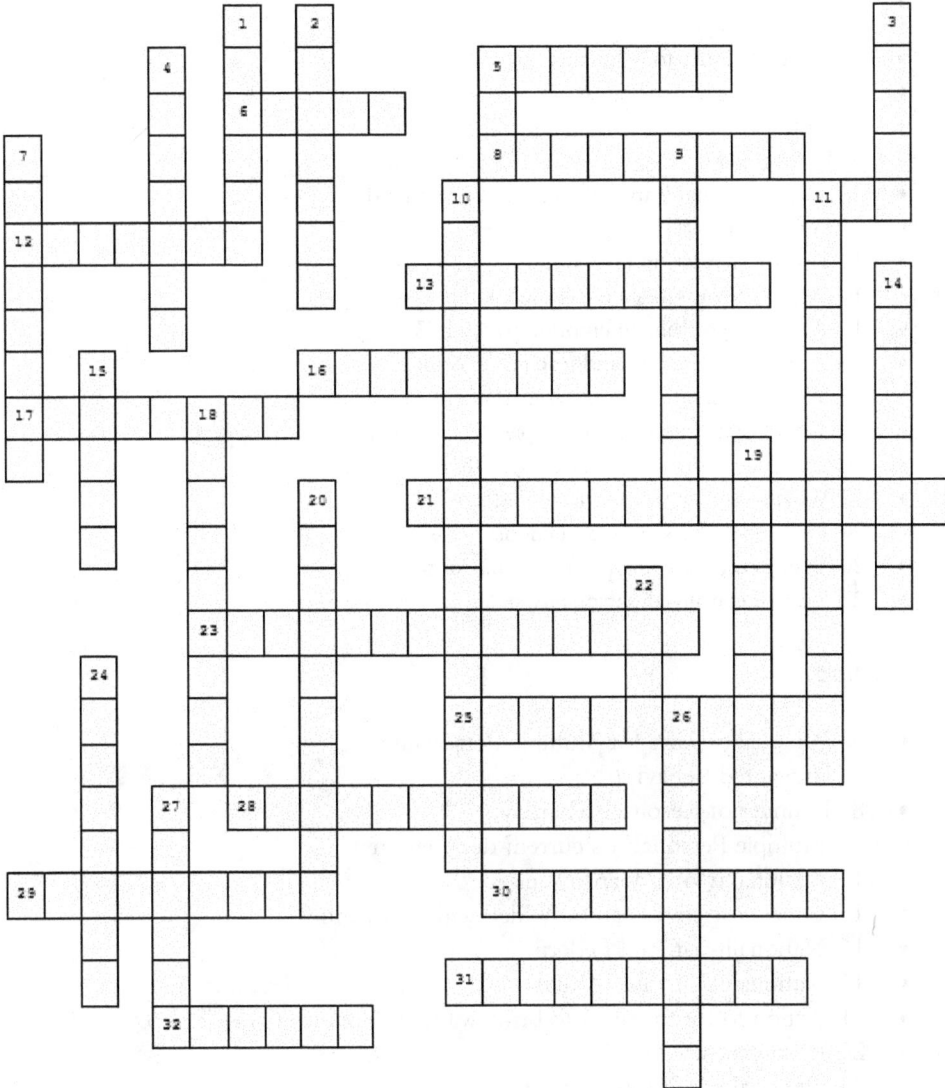

Down

- 1. Original Nationality of Helen Watkins
- 2. RT Techniques to help Clients
- 3. Emotionally upset States
- 4. They started Ego State Therapy
- 5. Helpful to know ___ of State at ISE to Bridge
- 7. Retro State that learned behavior in Childhood
- 9. Personality Parts
- 10. Resources rarely in the Conscious 9,6
- 11. What a depressed state is Vaded with
- 14. Action to go from an emotion to the ISE
- 15. A student of Federn and teacher of Watkins
- 18. What a ruminating state is Vaded with
- 19. What a state that feels unlovable is Vaded with
- 20. Two States that are fighting each other
- 22. What a state with a phobia is Vaded with
- 24. Retro State that causes addictions
- 26. Trains client to bring preferred state out
- 27. He first conceived personality states

Across

- 5. Personality Parts for Multiple Personality
- 6. Unwanted Behavior
- 8. Founder of Resource Therapy
- 11. Multiple Personality's current designation
- 12. Nationality of Edoardo Weiss
- 13. Usual time states can be Vaded with Confusion
- 16. Nationality of Paul Federn
- 17. Nationality of John Watkins
- 21. Action to for therapist to bring wanted state into Conscious 6,8
- 23. Resources used Daily 7,6
- 25. Nationality of Gordon Emmerson
- 28. Internalized Impressions
- 29. Usual time states can be Vaded with Rejection
- 30. Wrong Resource State in the Conscious
- 31. When a state is out and in control
- 32. Healthy Resource States

2 Day 2 - Conflicted States

Several RT Actions are overviewed during the second day's training. Actions 4 thru 7 are the Actions that bring a State Vaded with Fear or Rejection back into a Normal Condition. Action 8 is used to find the best Resource State to be Conscious at a particular time, and Action 11 is to bring conflicted states back to a Normal Condition.

The practice for Day 2 is to help you become comfortable with conflicted state negotiation. It is important that you learn when to use conflicted state negotiation and to be highly familiar with the negotiation steps. Each day of the training will move to new skills, so you should gain a good level of understanding for every practice so you will have that skill in your toolbox for clients.

A short definition of the day two terms is provided below. You should make sure you are comfortable with the fuller meaning of these terms by the end of this day's training.

2.1   Core Concepts for Day 2 Training

Page #'s are Hyperlinks on eBooks.		Page
Naming States	Each state should name itself, or agree with the suggested name.	49
Action 4 Expression	The most powerful Action to empower a state Vaded with Fear or Rejection.	51
Action 5 Introject Speak	Where the State Vaded with Rejection understands it was the Rejecting person who was unable to share unconditional love.	52

2.1 Core Concepts for Day 2 Training

Action 6 Removal	The Vaded State can choose if it wants another in its inner space.	54
Action 7 Relief	Bringing in a helping state, and renaming states that had negative names.	54
Finding a helping State	Techniques for finding a helping state for Action 7, Relief.	56
Action 8 Find Resource	Finds the best state for the client to have in the Conscious at a given time.	56
Action 11 Conflicted State Negotiation	Negotiation where Conflicted states learn to value each other, to communicate and to collaborate.	65
Action 12 Imagery Check	After intervention, the therapist returns the client to the image in Action 2, Vivify Specific, to insure that a difference experience is evident.	61
Sensory Experience Memory	An Emotional Memory that may or may not be Consciously connected to an intellectual memory.	62

2.1.1   Naming States

It is important to get a name for each Resource State that you work with. Often, when you ask the state you are speaking with, "What can I call you?" The state will give a name like, Protector, Afraid, or Head. Sometimes it is difficult for a state to come up with the name. When this happens it is fine to suggest some names that might be appropriate for the state, and it is fine if the state chooses one of those suggested names or comes up with an alternative.

It is imperative for a state to be able to name itself. Therefore, one should not ask one Resource State what is a good name for another Resource State. One should always make sure that the state is out and in the Conscious before asking for its name.

It is okay to accept a negative name for a Vaded state, such as, "Afraid," because that name fits the feeling of the state while it is Vaded and it most easily identifies with that feeling. Following resolution the state will no longer hold the negative feeling and then it can choose a new, positive, name that better reflects how it feels as it experiences a sense of safety and support.

When naming a Retro state it is best not to accept a name of the unwanted behavior of the state. It is better to accept a name that reflects the purpose of the state. For example, it would not be good to accept the name, 'Gambler', and it would be much better to accept the name, 'Escape'. The state that had used gambling as a means to accomplish its purpose of escaping will be able to find a new way of fulfilling its purpose if it is needed in the future. You can ask a state a question such as, "How have you helped this person in the past by gambling? The answer to a question like that will reflect the purpose of the state.

2.1.2   Action 4: Expression

When the State Vaded with Fear or Rejection is able to say absolutely anything it wants, within the imagery of the initial sensitizing event, it quickly learns that there is nothing internal that can

hurt it. It may at first feel too afraid to express its feelings, but with encouragement and assistance from the therapist it will be able to do so. It learns that no matter what it says, it is safe, and it learns that there is nothing that can hurt it internally. This is the most empowering RT Action.

During the expression phase the therapist may say things like:

- "This isn't really happening right now, so you can say anything you want."

- "We know we are in a therapy room right now, so it is safe to say exactly how you feel."

- "Is it okay if I tell him first?"

- "Let's just shrink him down to 1 inch tall. He's just tiny and has a squeaky little voice. Please don't step on him, because I want you to be able to tell him what you want to say."

Empowering statements such as these make it easier for the state that has been Vaded with Fear or Rejection to express itself.

2.1.3   Action 5 Introject Speak

Introjects are internalized impressions held by our Resource States. Just as an actor can take on the role of a person in a play or a movie, a Resource State can take on the role of an Introject, and speak as that Introject. This can be useful in therapy. The Resource State can gain a Sensory Experience Memory from having had the feelings of the Introject. When it returns to reflect on those feelings the Resource State can gain an 'AHA' understanding about the dynamics of the relationship.

Introject Speak can be done with the client's eyes closed (when working with States Vaded with Rejection). By applying the Introject Speak Action the client may hear from the Introject of a relative, friend, or even a deceased loved one.

When a Resource State is given the opportunity to speak as an Introject that Resource State is able to gain a deeper understanding of the dynamic between it and the Introject that it holds. For example, a Vaded State with Rejection may be asked to speak as the Introject of the person who it felt rejection from. Upon learning that this Introject was unable to share unconditional love because of its own difficulties a deeper understanding of the dynamic is made possible. Therefore, the state that had previously felt unlovable is able to gain the understanding that it was the Introject that was unable to share unconditional love at that point in time.

The first step in Introject Speak after Bridging to the Initial Sensitizing Event (with the clients eyes still closed) is to have the Resource State to say what it wants to say directly to the Introject (Expression). Next, the therapist can make a statement such as, "Right now I want to talk directly with dad. I want you to be like a great actor being dad. Just forget who you are so I can hear directly from dad and how he feels right now. Dad, your son has been very brave and has told you that he does not feel like you really love him. Dad, how does that make you feel, when you hear him say that?"

The purpose of Introject Speak is not to change the Introject, the internalized impression the Resource State has of the other person. The purpose is for the Resource State to gain a better understanding of the dynamic between the Introject and the state. If the Introject of a parent says, "My life is too difficult. I should never have had him," then the therapist should say, "Thank you for talking with me, mum. Thank you for being honest with me. Right now I want to talk with (The name of the Vaded State).

Gee, I can understand why you feel the way you do. Anyone would feel that way. Right now your mum is not able to share the love that every child deserves. Every child deserves unconditional love. I want to make sure that you get the love that every child deserves."

It is by assuming the identity of the Introject, and then returning to the Resource State, that the Resource State is able to gain a deeper understanding, through its Sensory Experience Memory of what it felt like to be the rejecting person. The Resource State remembers the feelings it had when it pretended to be the Introject, and this allows it to have a cathartic shift in understanding. There is a movement in understanding from, 'There is something wrong with me. I am unlovable,' to, 'That other person was not able to give the unconditional love that every child deserves.' This is a profound shift.

2.1.4   Action 6 Removal

Removal is very quick and easy, but is an important step. When working with states that have been Vaded with Fear or Rejection, once they have been empowered during the Expression Action, they will be able to decide if they want to allow the Introject to stay in their inner space. Remember, Introjects are Resource State specific, so if one Resource State tells an Introject it wants its space clear of it, that does not affect other Resources and their relationships with that Introject.

Following the Expression Action for an Introject Vaded with Fear, or following the Introject Speak Action for an Introject Vaded with Rejection, the therapist may say something like:

- "That was very good. Now, do you want (Introject name) to stay in your space, or do you want your space clear? It's up to you."

(If the Resource State says it can stay)

- "That's nice. You can just let it know that."

(If the Resource State says it wants it to leave)

- "Just go ahead and tell it to leave."

It does not matter whether the Resource State wants the Introject to remain in its space or wants the Introject to leave its space. What matters is that it understands that it has the choice. Understanding that it has the choice is an additional step that allows it to feel empowered in relation to the Introject.

2.1.5   Action 7 Relief

Following the empowering Actions of Expression and Removal, the final step in the resolution of States Vaded with Fear or Rejection is Relief. Relief is an important Action that leaves the previously Vaded Resource State feeling safe and supported.

This Action requires finding another Resource State that can stay with the previously Vaded State to make sure it feels safe and supported. The best way to find a Resource State that has this ability is to ask the client, by name, how he or she would support a loved one with the same description of the previously Vaded Resource State. For example:

1. **Find Helping State:**

   - "Amy, if you saw a five year old little girl who you know and care about who felt lost and alone, Amy, what would you want to do?"

When the client answers this question you can ask,

2. **Get a name for Helping State**

   - "What can I call this part of you that just responded?"

3. **Instruct Helping State**

Then, upon getting a response (such as, 'Helper') you can say,

   - "Helper, thank you for talking with me. I would like you to go to Hurt, right there in her room, put your arm around her and let love flow from you into every cell and fiber of her being. You can do this, Helper, and everything else you do. The more you do the more powerful you become. You can do many things all at once. Right now just go to Hurt and let her know that you will always be there for her. Let her know she will never, ever be alone."

4. **Rename previously Vaded State if it had a negative name**

Then I will ask,

   - "Hurt, how does that feel? (And with 'Hurt's' response) Hurt, it sounds to me like you are not feeling hurt anymore. What would be a better name that describes how you are feeling now? What would you like to be called now? (after the answer, e.g., Loved) That is a wonderful name. From now on I will call you, 'Loved'."

At the end of the Relief Action the client will be experiencing a very different affect than was experienced immediately following Bridging. The Resource State

that had been Vaded with Fear or Rejection has been changed to a state in a Normal Condition. It no longer holds negative emotions that can surface and cause the client anxiety.

2.1.6   Finding a helping State

What should you do when the client has difficulty finding a Resource State that can help another state?

If you are looking for one state to help another state to feel safe, loved, or strong, it is good to call the client by name, and ask the client, e.g., "Jenny, if you saw an eight-year-old child who you knew and loved upset in a room, what would you want to do, Jenny?" Then say, "What can I call this part of you that just answered my question?" By asking the client precisely how the client would like to help another person of the same age and need of the State, it is possible to find the client's best Resource State to be helpful.

If the client needs an assertive state it is good to ask the client when in the past has there been assertive behavior, then vivify specific that time and get a name for the state that can be assertive. If the client cannot remember ever being assertive, then ask the client to define what it would be like to be assertive. While the client is defining exactly what it would be like to be assertive ask, "What can I call this part I am talking with right now? Call that part by name and suggest, "It seems like you really have a good handle on assertiveness. This person needs a part that can be assertive. Since you understand assertiveness better than any other part, will you be the assertive part. You can help a lot." Parts like to help if they can, and a part that can describe assertiveness can be assertive.

2.1.7   Action 8: Find Resource

The Find Resource Action is different from the above, finding a helping state for a previously Vaded State.

The Find Resource Action is used to find a Resource State that is the best state for the client to use externally. For example, if a person wants to find their best resource to play a sport, or to write a paper this action would be appropriate. Often following the normalization of a Vaded State it is important to find the best Resource for the client to use when the Vaded State had come out previously. A client may benefit from finding a communicative state to be conscious when public speaking, once the frightened, childhood state is no longer vaded and jumping into the Conscious.

Find Resource is used to locate the best Resource that the client has for a specific time or activity. It is a straightforward Action, comprised of only two parts. First, a question is asked to determine how the client wants to experience this time or activity both internally and externally, and secondly the Vivifying Specific action is used to locate and name a Resource that can be available to the client. For example, if the client wants to locate a Resource that could better talk with her teenage son, the first question could be:

1. "When you are talking with him how do you want to experience the conversation? How do you want to act externally, and how do you want to feel internally?"

You will need to make sure that you get a response for both parts of this question. Then, ask the client when in the past she has been able to act this way and feel this way with anyone, at any time in her life.

2. Upon getting a response to that question use the Vivify Specific Action to find and name the helpful Resource State. Then, call that state by name, and ask it if it would be willing to help the client in the future during the times when it is needed.

When resources are asked to help, if they feel able to help, they are happy to do so. Resources love to be conscious and they love to help. It is more often the case that two resources want to be out at the same time, than no Resource State wants to be out.

What if the client does not have a Resource State that is needed?

If the client cannot remember a time when he or she was able to act and feel in the desired manner, it is necessary to find a Resource State that can practice and take on that ability. We are not building a new Resource State, merely finding one that has the ability to take on the needed characteristics. In order to find a state that can take on the needed characteristics, ask the client to describe what it would be like to be able to act and feel in the desired way. The Resource State that can answer this question will be able to practice, and take on the desired activity. For example: (the client has not been able to remember ever being assertive)

- "Amy, what would it be like to be assertive in the way you would like to be? Just describe how you would talk, how you would feel, and what that would be like for you."

(while getting this description)

- "What can I call this part that is talking right now? What can I call you, this part that really has a good handle on assertiveness?"

(Let's say the name given was 'Strong')

- "Strong, thank you for talking with me. It sounds to me like you have a really good understanding of assertive behavior. Amy needs an assertive part right now, and it seems like you are the best part to help Amy by taking on this behavior. The more you practice it the better you will get at it. Strong, would you be willing, when Amy needs you, to be her assertive part?"

A fragile part could never be assertive, but it will not be a fragile part that describes what it would be like to be assertive. The part that describes what it would be like to be assertive understands that ability well enough to be able to take it on.

2.1.8   Action 11: Conflicted State Negotiation

Conflicted Resources are those that have a pathological level of disagreement. For example, two states may disagree on having, or not having a dessert, but as long as a decision can be made without feeling a high level of anxiety the states are not considered to be conflicted. If one state wants to sleep and one state wants to think, and the conflict results in a high level of anxiety or a threat to good health then those states are Conflicted Resources and need Conflicted State Negotiation

Conflicted State Negotiation is a process of assisting the **Conflicted States** to learn to understand the value of each other, communicate directly, and learn to collaborate. Following this, states that were conflicted will be able to collaborate in the future as circumstances change.

Conflicted states are identified when the client makes statements like:

- I hate myself when I do that.

- I procrastinate.

- I don't know why I do that.

- I can't make myself do it.

- I try to sleep, but I just keep thinking.

- I embarrass myself.

- I can't control what I do.

The Table below outlines when it is appropriate to use this Action. Generally, the Conflicted State Negotiation Action is helpful to resolve emotional conflicts between two Resources, but when that emotional conflict is being fed by the pathology of a Vaded or Retro State, that pathology should first be resolved. The resolution of Vaded or Retro states most usually resolve conflict between them and another state. Therefore, Conflicted State Negotiation is not needed with Vaded or Retro States.

Table 10: When to use the Conflicted State Negotiation Action

Two states are in conflict and	Therapeutic Course re Conflicted State Negotiation Action
Neither is Retro or Vaded	Conflicted State Negotiation Action.
One is Vaded	Resolve the Vaded State
One is Retro Avoiding	Resolve the Vaded State, then Retro State Negotiation

One is Retro Original	Retro State Negotiation
Following the completion of any intervention, if two states are still in Emotional Conflict	Conflicted State Negotiation Action.

There are nine steps to moving Conflicted States to Normality: Situate two facing chairs with the client in one, looking toward the other.

1. With the client in one of the chairs use the Vivify Specific Action to ensure one of the **Conflicted States** is in the Conscious, and then get a name for that state.

2. Call it by name and ask it what it feels about the other state that it has been conflicted with in the past. Take notes detailing what it says.

3. Show understanding for its feelings, but make a case to it how important and useful the other state can be.

4. Ask the client to stand and switch chairs then speak directly with the other Conflicted State, making sure you get a name from it for itself.

5. Call it by name and ask it what it feels about the other state that it has been conflicted with in the past. Take notes detailing what it says.

6. Show understanding for its feelings, but make a case to it how important and useful the other state can be.

7. Continue making a case until the Conflicted State begins to understand the utility of the other state, then ask it to speak directly with the other state, saying how it understands its importance and how it wants to work together with it in the future with a specified plan of collaboration.

8. Again, have the client switch chairs and make sure the other state is able to respond in the same way, saying how it understands the other's importance and how it wants to work together with it in the future with a specified plan of collaboration.

9. Show appreciation to both states for working together and suggest that in the future as circumstances change they will be able to continue to work together and collaborate.

2.1.9   Action 12: Imagery Check

The Imagery Check Action is an excellent way to check the efficacy of therapeutic intervention, and to allow the client to gain practice, and to gain a confidence that the intervention has been effective. RT Action 2 (Vivify Specific) is used in all Resource Therapy interventions. Therefore, the therapist already has imagery, and notes about that imagery pertaining to the issue that the client was ready to change.

Imagery Check is merely returning to the imagery that was problematic when the client presented in therapy. This is the same imagery used in RT Action 2 (Vivify Specific) to bring the state needing change into the conscious. Imagery Check is to see if there has been a change in the client's experience within that imagery.

Look back at the notes you took during Vivify Specific so you can help the client back into the imagery that had been a problem in the past. The same types of questions and techniques that were used in Vivify Specific can be used during Imagery Check in order to assist the client to return to the original image. This normally occurs quite quickly because the client has already established an experience in achieving the imagery, and because the client is normally more focused during the later parts of the therapy session.

The Imagery Check Action is useful to demonstrate to the client that a change has been made, and as a check for the therapist that the right work was done. The client should have a more positive experience during Imagery Check than was experienced during the first Vivify Specific. If a more positive experience is not evident, then further work needs to be done to assist the Resource State that holds the problem.

2.1.10   Sensory Experience Memory

We often think of memory as only intellectual memory, our ability to mentally revisit a past event. I propose that along with our Intellectual Memory we also have a Sensory Experience Memory (SEM) that is the emotional re-experiencing of an event. Because SEM is core to many psychological issues and also key to resolving many issues it is important to gain an understanding of it.

Sensory Experience Memory (Emmerson, 2014) is the emotional re-experiencing of a past event. It may, or may not, be connected to an Intellectual Memory. For example, if a person witnesses a car accident, during the immediate re-telling of that event the person will often experience the SEM related to the accident. Here, the Intellectual Memory and the SEM are directly connected, and the person will feel the emotions experienced when retelling the accident that was witnessed. But, the SEM may become dissociated from the Intellectual Memory. For example, a person may experience a trauma in childhood, and if left unprocessed, that person can later re-experience the SEM associated to that trauma in adulthood in the form of anxiety, fear, feelings of unworthiness, or panic, without knowing where the unwanted emotions are coming from.

A SEM normally diminishes over time. As long as the person is able to talk about what was experienced, gain a perspective about it, and feel comfortable in moving forward, the Sensory Experience Memory of the incident will lessen over time and the person will become better able to recall the Intellectual Memory without feeling emotionally out of control. A trait of a SEM is that it naturally diminishes over time, when there has been conversations that help the person feel understood, therefore, fears, anger, and other negative emotions can diminish.

2.1.11   The nature of Sensory Experience Memories:

- They are the non-intellectual, emotional recall of an event
- They may or may not be connected to the Intellectual Memory (i.e., the person may not know where the feeling is coming from)
- They may be positive or negative
- They tend to extinguish over time, unless unprocessed
- They are the negative experiences of Vaded States
- They may be used in therapy to achieve understanding and change
- In order to experience a SEM the Resource that originally experienced it must hold the conscious

2.1.12   Examples of Sensory Experience Memories:

- Fears associated with Phobias
- Panic Attacks
- Anxiety that expresses beyond the current situation
- Feelings of low self-worth
- Depression
- Feelings of Confusion and Rumination

SEMs may be negative or positive, but sadly the negative SEMs last longer because they are the ones that require processing. It is probable that following a negative experience, SEMs are held so the person can learn something before letting go of what was experienced. A negative SEM can be held for a lifetime, re-emerging, causing the person to re-experience the negative feelings even when they are no longer associated with the original event.

2.1.13   How SEMs can be used in Therapy

The negative emotions experienced during a SEM can guide the therapist and client to the initial sensitizing event that caused that emotion. This both creates an intellectual understanding of where that emotion comes from and it provides an opportunity to process the emotion so the client can become empowered, safe and supported in relation to the event. The negative SEM is therefore extinguished and the client is left with the intellectual understanding of the event. This is how Vaded States are brought back to a state of Normality.

SEMs are also useful in helping clients with a number of other issues. When there is confusion relating to a present or past relationship, that confusion is most often the result of a sense of an 'unknowing' about how another person may feel. When the therapist has a client to speak with the Introject of the other person (living or dead) in an empty chair, then asks the client to go to that chair and reply as the other person, a SEM is created. The SEM is the emotional experience of being the Introject. When clients return from an Introject's chair they return with a SEM of the feelings of the Introject.

This SEM is more important than what the client said, while speaking from the Introject's chair. It is the client's experience of the emotions of the Introject that can provide a cathartic increase in understanding about the relationship. More succinctly, it is not as much what the Introject has said, as what the Introject felt that allows the client to experience a catharsis in understanding.

Conflicted Resource States are states that do not understand and appreciate the value of each other, e.g., a work state and a rest state. They can achieve an understanding of the value of each other with the use of SEMs. In the same way a client can gain a better understanding of another person with the use of properly directed empty chair work. Resource States can gain an appreciation and understanding of each other when they return to their chair holding the SEM of the state that just spoke from the other chair. SEMs often extinguish quickly, but they are still strong during the process of switching from one chair to the next. That means a state that has just spoken about needing rest and the importance of recharging the body can be felt by the state that wants to work constantly when the client moves back over to the worker state's chair. When states learn that each are important and each needs time, an inner peace can develop and states can respect each other and collaborate so each can help appropriately. Creating a conversation between states so they can learn the feelings of each other with the use of SEMs is a powerful technique.

2.2   Skills for Day 2

The skills that are to be practiced on Day 2 is Conflicted State Negotiation. The one specific use for this action is for working with two otherwise healthy states that are in conflict. The two most common presentations of Conflicted States are those of Work and Rest, or Work and Play and those for Sleep and Thinking.

States in conflict of Rest will often be associated with chronic fatigue. When a Rest state does not get enough time for an extended amount of time a lot of stress is placed on the body and this can result in a negative physiological response.

2.2.1   Conflicted State Practice

The steps are as follows:

Conflicted State Negotiation Practice: (Using two chairs)

1. Ensure one of the **Conflicted States** is in the Conscious, and then get a name for that state.
2. Call it by name and ask it what it feels about the other state.
3. Make a case to it how useful the other state can be.
4. Switch chairs and get a name from the other state for itself.
5. Ask it what it feels about the other state.
6. Make a case to it how useful the other state can be.
7. Ask it to speak directly with the other state, saying how it understands its importance and how it wants to work together with it.
8. Switch chairs and make sure the other state is able to respond in the same way, speaking directly to the other state.
9. Suggest that in the future as circumstances change they will be able to continue to work together and compromise.

For video examples go to www.tinyurl.com/learnresourcetherapy.

2.3 Quiz and Activities for Day 2

2.3.1 Quiz

1. When did states Vaded with Fear and Rejection normally become Vaded?

2. How should a therapist introduce working with empty chairs?

3. What if the client talks about the person in the other chair, rather than to that person?

4. What is the Expression Action used for?

5. When should the Introject Speak Action be used?

6. During which Action may a state be asked if it would like to change its name?

7. What question is asked during the Removal Action?

8. What is Sensory Experience Memory (SEM)?

9. What does SEM have to do with states Vaded with Fear or Confusion?

10. How can SEM be helpful during the therapeutic process?

2.3.2 Table Activity

Table 11: Fill in the table, explaining what to do in each instance.

Two states are in conflict and	Therapeutic Course re Conflicted State Negotiation Action
Neither is Retro or Vaded	

One is Vaded	
One is Retro Avoiding	
One is Retro Original	
Following the completion of any intervention, if two states are still in Emotional Conflict	

See Table 10: When to use the Conflicted State Negotiation Action, p. 59.

2.3.3　Day 2 Crossword

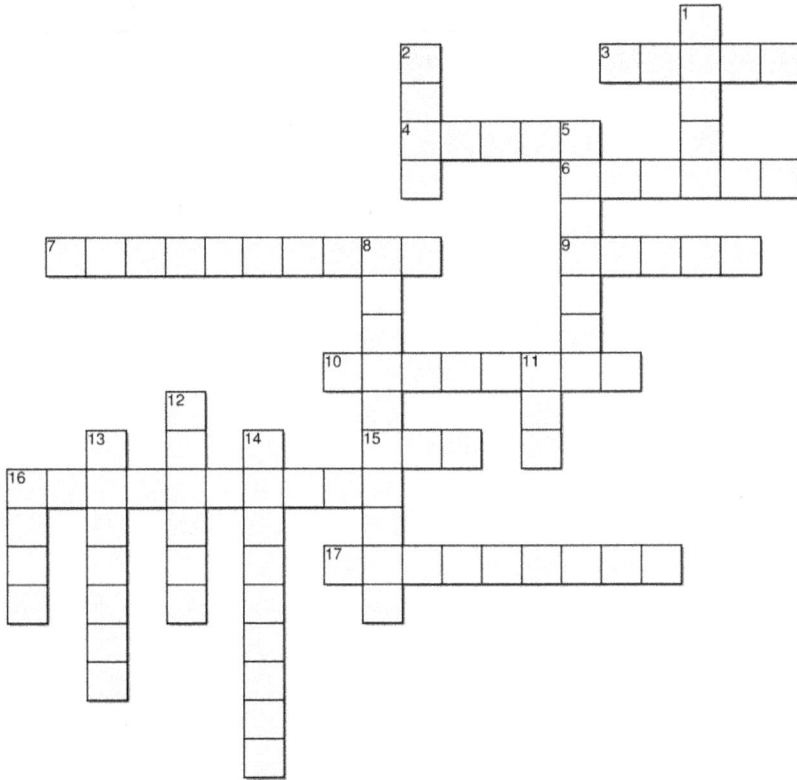

Across

- 3. ISE is the Initial Sensitizing ____
- 4. What you need from every Resource State you work with 1,4
- 6. SEM is the Sensory Experience ____
- 7. A state that does not like or understand another state
- 9. The number of steps in Bridging
- 10. The Action that comes before Expression
- 15. A good or bad emotional memory
- 16. Whose name is called when asking for a helping state? 3,7
- 17. A state is in the ____ when it picks or approves its name

Down

- 1. Name this state with its purpose not its behavior
- 2. Bridging is used for states vaded with __ or Rejection
- 5. After Bridging, rather than change the memory, we change the ____
- 8. The most empowering Action for to a State Vaded with Fear
- 11. Bridging moves from the unwanted emotion to the ____
- 12. Action when a Vaded State may get a new name
- 13. The Introject is told to stay or go in this Action
- 14. Introject Speak is used with a State Vaded with ...
- 16. Conflicted States both want to be Conscious at the same ____

3 Day 3 RT Diagnosis & Dissonant States

A main emphasis of Day 3 is Diagnosis. The 8 diagnostic categories are looked at in some detail. If you spend some time becoming comfortable with the 8 pathologies you will find diagnosis straightforward. It is helpful to be able to diagnose quickly during therapy when a statement or an emotion reveals a pathology.

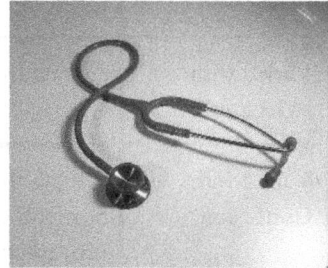

Day 3 also has a focus on working with Dissonant States. These are states that are out at the wrong time. They feel uncomfortable being out and are happy when a more appropriate state can take over.

Dissonant States are the easiest states to work with, as they don't want to be out at the time that is problematic. The Actions that are used for assisting a Dissonant State to Normal State behavior have already been covered, Action 2, Vivify Specific, Action 8, Find Resource, and Action 12, Imagery Check. The practice for Day 3 is for the student to become comfortable working with Dissonant States.

A short definition of the day three terms is provided below. You should make sure you are comfortable with the fuller meaning of these terms by the end of this day's training.

3.1 Core Concepts for Day 3 Training

Page #'s are Hyperlinks on eBooks.		Page
Action 1 Diagnosis	The state that needs change is located and diagnosed into one of the 8 pathologies.	73

3.1 Core Concepts for Day 3 Training

Page #'s are Hyperlinks on eBooks.		Page
Vaded with Fear	A state that is carrying unresolved fear from an ISE.	78
Vaded with Rejection	A state that feels unlovable or unworthy.	80
Vaded with Confusion	A state that can't stop ruminating about something. Sometimes guilt, shame, or blame. Can be an inability to move forward.	82
Vaded with Disappointment	A sad state that is so disappointed it blocks other states from positive activity. This state causes psychological depression.	83
Retro Original	An unwanted behavior that was learned in childhood while the state was forming.	84
Retro Avoiding	An unwanted behavior that is to help avoid the bad feelings of a state Vaded with Fear or Rejection.	85
Conflicted	A state that does not appreciate another state and is in conflict with it.	88
Dissonant	A healthy state that is conscious at the wrong time. Feels incompetent.	90
A Dissonant vs. a Retro State	A Dissonant state does not want to be out, while a Retro state does.	91

3.1.1   Diagnosis: Action 1

The goal of RT Diagnosis is to classify the presented issue into one of eight categories, see Table 12, Table 13, and Table 15. Almost all clients present with some sort of anxiety. Below are the tables to overview diagnosis, and then each diagnosis is described in more detail.

Table 12: RT Classification Flowchart

1. What is the presenting concern?	2. The Resource might be:	3. When Conscious it feels	4. Has been noticed since Childhood?	5. Diagnostic Classification
Unwanted Behavior	Retro Original	Feels competent	Yes →	Retro Original
	Retro Avoiding		No →	Retro Avoiding
	Dissonant	Feels incompetent →		Dissonant
Unwanted Emotion (Vaded)	Fear	Fear →		V/ Fear
	Rejection	Not good enough →		V/Rejection
	Disappointment	Low Energy →		V/Disappointment
	Confusion	Ruminates →		V/Confusion
Internal Conflict	Conflicted	In conflict with another state →		Conflicted

Table 13: Pathological Resource States

	Pathology of State	**Characterisation**
4 Vaded Categories (Unwanted emotions)	Vaded with Fear	When Conscious has anxiety or emotions based on fear.
	Vaded with Rejection	When Conscious has anxiety or emotions based on feeling unlovable or not good enough.
	Vaded with Disappointment	Has low energy and one Resource refuses to allow other Resources enjoyment.
	Vaded with Confusion	Rumination, guilt, or shame.
2 Retro Categories (Unwanted behaviors)	Retro Original	Displays unwanted behavior that has been evident since childhood.
	Retro Avoiding	Displays unwanted addictive or OCD behavior. This avoids the vaded feelings of Fear or Rejection
	Conflicted	Two states want the Conscious at the same time or two states disagree on a major issue.
	Dissonant	The state that is Conscious does not want to be out and another state would be preferred.

Table 14 : How Pathological Resource States feel and how they are reported by other states

Pathology	When Conscious it Feels	Other States report that it...
Vaded with Fear	Anxiety or emotions based on fear.	Other states will wish these states would just go away and stop interfering with emotions that get in their way. They attempt to push the emotions away.
Vaded with Rejection	Unlovable or not good enough.	
Vaded with Disappointment	Disheartened and sad. It has low energy.	Other states are blocked by it. No state can have a good time.
Vaded with Confusion	Unable to let something go. Sometimes it feels guilt or blame.	They can't concentrate, work, or sleep because of the state's rumination.
Retro Original	Good about what they do. 'Stay out of my way.'	Other states feel these states get them in trouble. They don't like what they do and they cannot figure out how to stop them. They see them as out of control.
Retro Avoiding		
Conflicted	They feel like they are in a struggle. Will often report an inability to settle.	Other states are aware of the conflict and are frustrated by problems caused by the conflict.
Dissonant	The state that is out does not want to be out and another state would be preferred.	Other states are frustrated by the lack of competence it displays when Conscious.

Diagnosis is the Key to the session. In Resource Therapy there may be a number of diagnoses for different pathological states during the same session. The diagnosis is for a state, not for the entire person. It is more rare for a client to have only a single pathological state than to have a few states that need change. Direction for the session will be set by what the client is most ready to change.

Table 15: Pathologies Associated with each Classification Type

Classification	Associated Pathologies		
Vaded with Fear	Nightmares and sleep terror Specific Phobia Panic attack PTSD Agoraphobia Self-harming behavior Generalized Anxiety Disorder	Pathological Gambling Addictions Workaholism OCD (or Vaded with Rejection) Social Phobia (or Vaded with Rejection) Business Phobia (or Vaded with Rejection)	Compulsive Shopping (or more often is Vaded with Rejection) Antisocial (or Retro or Vaded with Rejection) Crisis reaction Dissociative Identity Disorders
Vaded with Rejection	Social Phobia (or Vaded with fear) Business Phobia (or Vaded with Fear) Narcissism Anorexia Nervosa Bulimia Nervosa	Antisocial (or Vaded with Fear) Feeling Unlovable Business Phobia (or Vaded with Fear) Compulsive Shopping (or Vaded with Fear) Over-competiveness	

Classification	Associated Pathologies		
Vaded with Confusion	Complicated Bereavement Rumination (over the welfare of others, death, or an event)	Existential angst Deep confusion over the breakdown of a relationship Guilt or Shame	
Vaded with Disappointment	Depression Relationship blame	Prolonged and intense feelings of loss	
Retro Original	Anti-Social Behavior Withdrawal Pouting	Rage Personality Disorders Passive Aggressive Behavior	
Retro Avoiding	Addictions Self-harming behavior Obsessive behavior (shopping, eating, work)	Anger or Rage as a means to act out Eating Disorders Work/relationship avoidance OCD	Shopping Addiction 'Perfectionistic' behavior Drug Taking Self-Harming behavior
Conflicted States	Procrastination Sleep Disturbance	Chronic Fatigue Cognitive Dissonance	
Dissonant State	Frustration in coping ability Feelings of ineptitude Inability to be real self	Writers block Sporting slumps Below par performance	

The precise diagnosis for a state may not become completely clear before RT Action 2. For example, if the client presents with anxiety over taking on a new job, it may not be clear whether this anxiety comes from a State Vaded with Fear or a State Vaded with Rejection. When this state is brought to the conscious using RT Action 2, Vivify Specific, and is able to express the emotions it is experiencing, it will then become clear if it is afraid, or if it has feelings of not being good enough.

3.1.2   Vaded with Fear

Resource States Vaded with Fear carry the illusion that the past is still happening. They are still afraid of something from the past. Therefore, the therapeutic interventions for these states make it clear to them that they are now safe, and that the past is not happening. Once these states feel safe and supported, once they are no longer the harbingers of fear, then they no longer interfere in the current life of the client.

A client example of a State Vaded with Fear will illustrate how this occurs. Jane presented with panic attacks. She said during her panic attacks she felt like she had to get away, or she might die. She said she felt like she needed to pull something away from her throat so she could breathe. And, she said she saw a color she described as 'blue but black'. She did not know why she had panic attacks, and she did not know why she felt the way she did when they occurred.

Bridging (RT Action 3) placed Jane back into her memory of the initial sensitizing event. She was 10 years old, swimming in the ocean, caught in an ocean riptide with her little cousin hanging onto her neck keeping her from being able to breathe properly. Her head would dip into the water and she would see the color 'blue but black'. She thought that she would die if she could not get out.

It is obvious that the emotions Jane's Resource State that was Vaded with Fear felt during panic attacks were a direct reflection of her experience during the initial sensitizing event. Jane's 10-year-old Resource State continued to carry the feeling that its life was in danger. It continued to carry the feeling of panic, therefore when this state came into the conscious Jane would experience panic.

As long as Jane's 10-year-old Resource State carried that feeling of panic it would be able to interfere in her life. It would do no good to focus on the times when Jane had panic attacks, because they were just a symptom of the fearful emotions held by Jane's 10-year-old state.

RT Actions allow the therapist to diagnose Resource States Vaded with fear and to bring resolution to those states so they no longer hold that fear. Resource States Vaded with fear can cause the following pathologies, among others.

Resources Vaded with Fear can cause these Pathologies

- Nightmares and sleep terror
- Specific Phobia
- Panic attack
- PTSD
- Agoraphobia
- Self-harming behavior
- Generalized Anxiety Disorder
- Dissociative Identity Disorders
- Pathological Gambling
- Addictions
- Workaholism
- OCD (or may be Vaded with Rejection)
- Social Phobia (or may be Vaded with Rejection)
- Business Phobia (or may be Vaded with Rejection)
- Compulsive Shopping (or more often is Vaded with Rejection)
- Antisocial (or may be Retro or Vaded with Rejection)
- Crisis reaction (benefitting from crisis intervention)

The Resource Vaded with Fear	The Normal State
A Resource Vaded with Fear feels there is something that can hurt it that has more power than it does. It prevents the client from living freely.	Normal States enjoy being in the Conscious. They focus on what is around them, not on a negative feeling.

Prior to the initial sensitizing event, States Vaded with Fear were in a normal condition, and they each had a role, a skill that they offered the personality. While traumatized with fear these states are not able to conduct their original purpose. Following resolution they will again be able to conduct their original purpose, therefore, clients will often describe a re-engagement with activities such as lighthearted play, or nurturance.

3.1.3   Vaded with Rejection

The most common issue I notice with clients presenting for therapy is Resource States Vaded with Rejection. A client having a Resource State Vaded with Rejection will report things like:

- I only feel good about myself when I please others
- If I disappoint someone else I feel terrible
- I feel like a fake
- I feel like if other people really knew me they would not like me
- I'm afraid to start the job because I might not be good enough
- I feel unlovable
- I have to fight to get approval

The Resource Vaded with Rejection	The Normal State
A Resource Vaded with Rejection feels it is unlovable, or not good enough. It can keep the client from engaging, and can cause the client to question personal value.	Normal States have positive feelings about themselves. They enjoy the time they have in the Conscious and feel they have something to offer.

The underlying common feature of Resource States Vaded with Rejection is a feeling of not being good enough, or not being lovable. These states are the cause of, or are central to, the following pathologies:

80

Resources Vaded with Rejection can cause these Pathologies

- Social Phobia (or may be Vaded with Fear)
- Business Phobia (or may be Vaded with Fear)
- Narcissism
- Anorexia Nervosa
- Bulimia Nervosa
- Antisocial (or may be Vaded with Fear)
- Feeling Unlovable
- Business Phobia (or may be Vaded with Fear)
- Compulsive Shopping (or may be Vaded with Fear)
- Over-competiveness

Resource States Vaded with Rejection have had an experience where they felt unworthy, incapable, or unlovable. The truth is all children deserve unconditional love. Resource States that feel unlovable continue to hold their negative feeling because they also continue to hold an impression of a person rejecting them. They have felt unloved, or unappreciated by someone else. Therefore, an important aspect of the treatment for Resources Vaded with Rejection is for the states to learn that all children deserve unconditional love, and if they did not receive what all children deserve, that is not the fault of the child.

Of course, this is something that cannot be intellectually transmitted. It is important for the Resource State Vaded with Rejection to return to the initial sensitizing event, then to speak as the rejecting Introject so an emotional understanding can be obtained. That emotional understanding is that at that point in time the Introject was not good at showing unconditional love. This does not mean that the Introject was bad, but it does shift the understanding from, 'I am unlovable', to 'The other person was not able to show me the love that all children deserve'.

The aim is for the part that felt rejected to learn that it was the other person who was, at that moment, unable to show unconditional love, to learn that it is lovable, and for it to experience getting unconditional love from a loving part of the client. It is necessary for the Vaded State to be conscious during treatment.

3.1.4   Vaded with Confusion

A Resource State Vaded with Confusion ruminates. This is when the client cannot let a thought go. It keeps returning. This can be confusion about, among other things, why someone committed suicide, how someone felt at the time of their death, what happened to an adopted child, guilt, shame, blame, the actions of another, or the actions of self.

The client with a Resource State Vaded with Confusion will often have difficulty sleeping. When they attempt to go to sleep the confused Resource State will often take over the conscious.

3.1.5   Vaded with Confusion

Resources Vaded with Confusion can cause these Pathologies

- Complicated Bereavement
- Rumination (over the welfare of others, death, or an event)
- Guilt or Shame
- Existential angst
- Deep confusion over the breakdown of a relationship

The Resource Vaded with Confusion	The Normal State
A Resource Vaded with Confusion cannot let something go. There is a rumination about confusion, blame, guilt or shame. Often there is an inability to sleep.	Normal States can let the past be past. They have an ability to experience the present. They have a backward peace and a forward vision.

The difference between a State Vaded with Confusion and a State Vaded

with Disappointment

There is a difference between being confused about the breakdown of a relationship, and being depressed about the breakdown of a relationship. The Resource State Vaded with Disappointment, the depressed state, will experience low levels of energy, and will block other states from enjoying aspects of living.

The client with a State Vaded with Confusion may be able to have energy at work, and other places. It will not block other Resource States from enjoying things. A person with a State Vaded with Confusion may do well during certain parts of the day, but will ruminate when the confused state is conscious.

3.1.6 Vaded with Disappointment

Resource States Vaded with Disappointment are upset that life is not how it was planned, or how it was preferred. These states are so upset that they block other states from participating in life in a positive way. They have lost their mission, the thing they felt was most important.

Key

One example is the person who discovered their partner was having an affair. A Resource State can be so disappointed that it will block any other states from enjoying the relationship.

Another example is the person who was fired from a long time job. This Resource State may be so disappointed that it will not allow any other resources to enjoy living. This can, over time, cause psychological depression.

3.1.7 Vaded with Disappointment

Resources Vaded with Disappointment can cause these Pathologies

- Depression
- Relationship blame
- Prolonged and intense feelings of loss

The Resource Vaded with Disappointment	The Normal State
A Resource Vaded with Disappointment feels low energy, upset, and unwilling for other parts of the personality to be happy.	Normal States enjoy the time they are out and they are thankful for the other states that can help out in various ways. They celebrate the happiness of other states.

It is imperative to understand that it is the interpretation of the event that is important, not actually what happened. Two individuals can experience the same event and one can become depressed, without the other being significantly bothered. The loss of a pet to one person may be an annoyance or even a relief, while to another person it may be devastating.

Therefore, the therapist should always show empathetic understanding to the Resource State that is Vaded with Disappointment. It is only when this Resource State feels understood that it will be cooperative during the therapeutic process.

3.1.8   Retro Original

Resource States are formed primarily during childhood when coping skills were practiced. A coping skill returned to over and over again that works for the person will become a Resource State. Sometimes the Resource State develops a coping skill that later becomes disliked by other personality parts. This is called a Retro State, a state that carries out activity that is not appreciated by other parts. When the original coping skill that formed a Resource State becomes disliked by other parts this is termed a Retro Original State. Examples of the Retro Original State are pouting, withdrawal, rage, and other antisocial behaviors.

It is possible for a person to exhibit annoying behavior and feel quite pleased with their behavior. This can be termed an annoying neighbor. This is not Retro State behavior. Behavior only becomes retro when that behavior becomes disliked by other personality parts.

Retro Original States can cause these Pathologies

- Anti-Social Behavior
- Withdrawal
- Pouting
- Rage
- Personality Disorders
- Passive Aggressive Behavior

Retro Original Resource States	The Normal State
Retro Original Resource States feel they have an important role to play. They do what they know how to do, and they really do not care if other states do not like what they do.	Normal States carry out behaviors that they feel is important and that other states also appreciate.

The behavior of Retro Original States is behavior that has been conducted by the client for as long as the client can remember. It is sometimes the case that a therapist can see behavior that the therapist would like changed, but unless this behavior is recognized by personality parts of the client as being unwanted, there is little value in focusing on changing that behavior.

3.1.9   Retro Avoiding

Retro Avoiding States overdo a behavior, like gambling, to help the person avoid having bad feelings. They normally start their avoiding behavior in adulthood. They are actually very good at helping the person avoid the upset feelings of States Vaded with Fear or Rejection. For example, the OCD person who checks locks and taps most nights before going to bed has found it more comfortable to be zoned into lock checking, than feeling anxiety. Because this lock checking behavior serves the purpose of protecting the person from unwanted emotions, it may be returned to more and more often. When the person loses an ability to stop the behavior, it has become a Retro Avoiding Behavior.

Retro Avoiding Behavior includes all psychological addictions and other avoiding behavior that is not able to be controlled by the client. The Retro Avoiding State has a purpose to protect the personality from the unwanted feelings of fear or rejection.

Retro Avoiding Pathologies

- Addictions
- OCD
- Self-harming behavior
- Obsessive behavior (shopping, eating, work)
- Uncontrolled Drug Taking
- Anger or Rage as a means to act out
- Eating Disorders
- Work/relationship avoidance
- Shopping Addiction
- 'Perfectionistic' behavior
- Self-Harming behavior

The state that comes to therapy

The State that initially presents to the therapist is not the Retro Avoiding State. The client with a Retro Avoiding State will almost always report to the therapist that a lack of control is the problem (i.e., drug taking, OCD, addictions, shopping, eating disorders, etc.).

The Resource State that originally presents in therapy feels a lack of control. This reporting state does not like the behavior that it cannot stop, therefore it sees this behavior as out of control. It feels out of control because the Retro State has control.

How the Retro Avoiding State feels

The actual Retro Avoiding State feels very much in control while it holds the Conscious.

Let's look at an example. Mandy comes home from work to an empty house and begins to feel alone and frightened. These are the feelings of a Vaded State. A Retro Avoiding State has learned how to help Mandy avoid these feelings. It takes over the Conscious, goes to the fridge and eats for the next 45 minutes, holding the Conscious firmly by causing Mandy to feel somewhat 'zoned out'. Other states are blocked during this time, and may even be surprised at Mandy's behavior when they return to the Conscious.

The Retro Avoiding State has become very good at making the personality feel safe during its behavior, in order to avoid the negative feelings of the Vaded State. The Retro State is very much in control, and it feels very useful.

Retro Avoiding Resource States	The Normal State
Retro Avoiding States feel they have an important role to play. They are happy to do what other states do not like if it saves the personality from having negative feelings.	Normal States carry out behavior that they feel is important and that other states appreciate also. They are at peace with other states, and will alter their behavior to bring it in line with the values of other personality parts.

It is almost impossible to cease Retro Avoiding Behavior without first attending to the upset feelings that are being avoided. It is of little value to work with the Retro Avoiding State until the Vaded State has returned to normality.

The process of helping the Retro Avoiding State cease its unwanted behavior is to first resolve the associated Vaded State, and second, to work directly with the Retro Avoiding State to ensure that, if it is needed again in the future, it can help with a behavior that is seen as positive.

3.1.10 Conflicted States

Conflicted States are in conflict over a decision or over activities. Imagine coming home from work and thinking about some extra work you need to get done during the evening. Then you find yourself watching TV, feeling a bit guilty, and hearing a little voice in your head saying, "You are lazy." You ignore the voice and continue watching TV, but the voice keeps going. This is an example of Conflicted States.

Both states are good, the body needs time out to rest and recover, and we need to get work done. The problem is that these two states may not understand the value of each other. The work state may see the rest state as lazy, and the rest state may see the work state as a slave driver.

Another example of Conflicted States are the two states that cannot agree over a major decision. One state says, "This relationship is not good for me. I deserve better. This is not the kind of relationship I want to have as I grow older." Another state says, "Commitment is important. Family stability is important. There are bad years in a good relationship. Let's just give this more time."

Here, these two states are conflicted and again need to learn both to value the contribution of the other, and learn to better communicate so major decisions can be made with less conflict.

3.1.11 Conflicted States Pathologies

- Procrastination
- Sleep Disturbance
- Chronic Fatigue
- Cognitive Dissonance

Conflicted Resource States	The Normal State
Conflicted Resource States do not understand the importance of other states. They either fight with them to be Conscious, or fight with them to win a decision.	Normal States respect other states and consider what they have to say. They work in a way to compromise with time so all states get the time they need.

We want our states to have different opinions on things and we want them to have different skills. Their diversity enables us to be multi-skilled. We do not want our states to fail to see the value of each other, to fight over which will hold the Conscious, or to discount the values or opinions of other states. Resource Therapy uses Conflicted State Negotiation to assist states to value and honor each other, and to learn to compromise in an ongoing manner.

Difference between Conflicted States and Retro and Vaded States

It is important to understand that Retro States will always have at least one other state that does not like what they are doing, and Vaded States will also have at least one other state that does not like its emotion interfering with life. These could be thought of as a one-way conflict, but this conflict is dispelled when the Retro or Vaded state returns to normality. Conflicted State Negotiation will not work with these Retro or Vaded States, and it does not need to. The interventions for these pathologies ends the conflict other states feel toward them. Conflicted States are otherwise Normal States, if not for the conflict they feel for each other. A work state and a rest state my both be useful and healthy states, except for lack of understanding and communication.

3.1.12 Dissonant States

Dissonant States do not like being out during the times when they are dissonant. They don't want to be there. They are not the best state to handle the situation.

Dissonant States respond very differently than Vaded States. Vaded States are tender parts of the psyche. They hold unresolved emotion. When they come to the Conscious they bring emotion from the past, emotion that does not match the current situation. Dissonant States do not hold unresolved emotion from the past. They would be normal states if they were not out at the wrong time. They understand they are not doing well in the moment, but they feel like they can't escape the moment.

Examples of Dissonant States include attempting to play a sport and feeling unable to perform as well as you normally would, or taking an exam and not remembering things that were learned.

3.1.13 Dissonant State Pathologies

- Frustration in coping ability
- Feelings of ineptitude
- Inability to be real self
- Writers block
- Sporting slumps
- Below par performance

Dissonant States should not be confused with Vaded States. Clients who relate higher levels of emotion when describing difficult situations most likely have Vaded States. Clients with Vaded States will not be able to merely find a more preferred state to bring into the Conscious, because the emotions of Vaded States can be very powerful. If a Vaded State is evident, it should be resolved using RT Actions 2 to 7.

Dissonant Resource States	The Normal State
Dissonant Resource States do not feel comfortable when Conscious. They do not like what they have to do when they are in the Conscious, and are frustrated with their ability.	Normal States enjoy their time out. When Conscious, they feel they are the best personality part for that moment. They may want to improve, but they feel able to do that.

The Dissonant State will be happy to allow another state to take the Conscious, once a better state is found to do that. The process of helping a Dissonant State return to normality (that is, come into the conscious only when it is the best state for the time) is to assist the client to define exactly the preferred manner to handle the situation, and then to find their best Resource that can do that (Find Resource). A final step is often to use Anchoring (RT Action 15) to make sure the client will be able to bring the preferred state to the conscious when desired.

3.1.14   Dissonant State vs a Retro State

A Dissonant State does not like to be out, and feels uncomfortable when it is out, and will be happy for another Resource State to take over. When the client is experiencing a Dissonant State in the Conscious there is a feeling of incompetence or a sense of 'this is such a waste of time'.

A Retro State is in complete control when it is out. It feels it has to be out, that it has an important job to do, and it is in complete control. It will block other states from the Conscious. Examples include a gambling state that will not allow a doubting state to enter, or a pathological eating state that will not allow another state to question what is being eaten.

Often, after a Retro State has been out the client will report being out of control. What the client is saying is that no other state could take control from the Retro State. The Retro state was in complete control.

3.2 Skills for Day 3

The skills the student should learn in Day 3 training is to diagnose the pathological state and to resolve a Dissonant State. A Dissonant State is the easiest pathology to resolve, because it does not want to be out.

Practice: After finding a Dissonant State

3.2.1 Resolving a Dissonant State Issue

1. Vivify Specific the time presented.
2. Ask for preferred internal/external experience,
3. Find a state that can do this (Find Resource),
4. Vivify Specific that state and get a state name,
5. Ask it for help
6. Ask original state if it is happy for the new state to take over during uncomfortable times
7. Imagery Check

For video examples go to www.tinyurl.com/learnresourcetherapy.

3.3 Quiz and Activities for Day 3

3.3.1 Quiz

1. What two questions are asked when using the Find Resource Action in order to locate a preferred Resource?

2. When the client cannot remember a time that their preferred Resource was conscious, what can the therapist do?

3. What type of State ruminates?

4. Pouting is an example of the behavior of what type of pathological state?

5. PTSD is an example of what type of pathological state?

6. Feelings of being unworthy, or not good enough are an example of what type of pathological state?

7. What type of pathological state is only pathological in that it is the wrong state to be out at a certain time?

8. What is the Imagery Check Action used for?

9. How many types of pathological Resource states are there?

10. Gambling is an example of what type of pathological state?

3.3.2 Day 3 Crossword

All answers are either Dissonant, Conflicted, (Vaded) Fear, Rejection, Confusion, Disappointment, (Retro) Original, or Avoiding

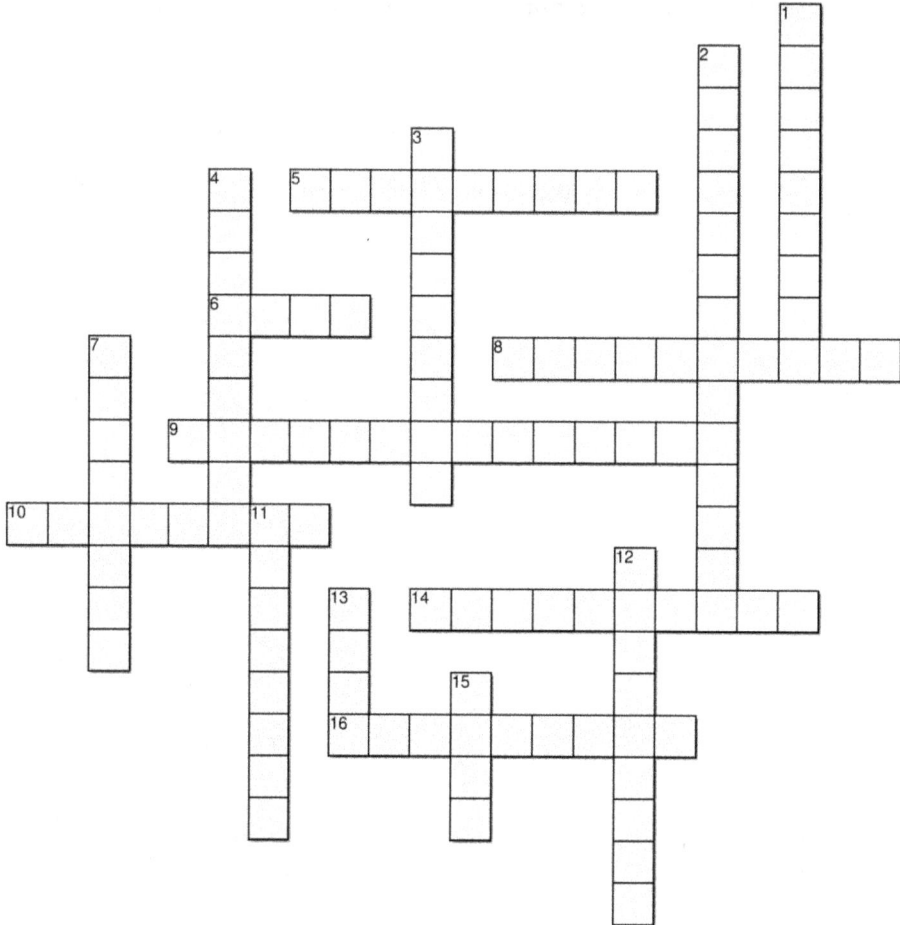

Across

- 5. I am anorexic.
- 6. I want to sleep, but I feel a lot of anxiety.
- 8. I procrastinate.
- 9. Since my partner died I don't feel like doing anything.
- 10. I withdraw when things are hard.
- 14. I am lazy and I need to get work done.
- 16. I'm afraid people will laugh at me.

Down

- 1. I want to sleep, but I just think about things instead.
- 2. There is no part of me that wants to do anything.
- 3. I get really upset when he criticizes me.
- 4. I can't get what he did out of my head. It even keeps me up at night.
- 7. My rage is really out of control.
- 11. I work day and night and can't stop.
- 12. When I try to study, I just think about other things I would like to do.
- 13. I have night terrors.
- 15. I have panic attacks.

3.3.3   Activity

Answer the following questions using the same 8 responses

1. When my boss criticizes me I just feel like crawling in a hole. _____
2. I know it is safe, but I can't get on an elevator. _____
3. I shop way too much. _____
4. I think I love him, but I get scared and pull back. _____
5. I am out of control with my gambling. _____
6. I have OCD. _____
7. I am not playing my sport as good as I know I can. _____
8. I am self-harming. _____

9. I keep thinking about the accident that killed her. _____
10. I am afraid of the dark. _____
11. I have a lot of anxiety when I am in a group. _____
12. Sometimes I speak well and sometimes I just want to. _____
13. People don't give me a chance. _____
14. When I am criticised I get angry. _____

4 Day 4 States Vaded with Confusion

A main emphasis of Day 4 is to learn to help clients stop ruminating. Clients with States Vaded with Confusion will not be able to stop thinking about something that they did, or that someone else did, or failed to do. Action 9, The Changing Chairs Introject Action is the key intervention for this issue.

Also covered on Day 4 are issues surrounding loss and grief. A distinction is made between normal grieving and complicated grieving, and techniques are presented to assist clients to become able to proceed through their grieving process in a healthy manner.

A short definition of the day four terms is provided below. You should make sure you are comfortable with the fuller meaning of these terms by the end of this day's training.

4.1 Core Concepts for Day 4 Training

Page #'s are Hyperlinks on eBooks.		Page
Vaded with Confusion vs. Vaded with Disappointment	A State Vaded with Confusion ruminates and does not block energy from other states. The Client can enjoy other states. A State Vaded with Disappointment feels low and blocks other states from enjoyment.	98
Working with a State Vaded with Confusion	This state needs to gain an internal sense of understanding, and it gets this with the Changing Chairs Introject Action.	99

Action 9 The Changing Chairs Introject Action	This action results in heightened understanding through the experience of feeling the emotions of the Introject.	99
Importance of Sensory Experience Memory in this Action	It is what the client feels, while speaking as the Introject, not what is said, that gives the sense of understanding.	101
Loss and Grief	It is normal to feel sad and grieve but heavy emotions block the process.	102
Heavy Emotions	Someone did something wrong emotions, including guilt and blame.	104

4.1.1 Vaded with Confusion vs Disappointment

Resources Vaded with Confusion have experienced an initial sensitizing event that they cannot incorporate into their understanding. This Resource is left with a fundamental and profound level of confusion, and its response to this lack of ability to understand, is a profoundly uncomfortable unknowing. While Resources Vaded with Disappointment hold a distinctly negative emotion, Resources Vaded with Confusion exhibit emotion about what is not known. Like Resources Vaded with Disappointment, they may affect the energy of other Resources, but when they do, this is at a much lower level. They may exhibit symptoms of rumination, existential angst, complicated bereavement, or withdrawal following a breakdown of the relationship, loss of job, or other losses. Clients with these types of Resources report being unable to stop ruminating about what they do not know.

Common to Resources Vaded with Confusion is an unfinished yearning for understanding. While a resource Vaded with Disappointment suffers because reality is not what was expected, a resource Vaded with Confusion suffers because it cannot make sense of what has happened or suffers because it does not know something that it has a great need to understand. Like all Vaded States, it suffers emotionally.

4.1.2 Working with a State Vaded with Confusion

Resolving a State Vaded with Confusion is a 4 step process employing Actions 1, 2, 9, and 12.

1. **Recognize a Confused Resource exists:** There must be a determination that the Vaded State suffers from confusion, as characterized by it experiencing overwhelming feelings of confusion with an out of control anxiety or a lack of ability to understand something of profound significance. (Action 1 – Identify Pathology, see page 73)

2. **Bring the confused Resource into the Conscious:** The Resource suffering confusion should be brought into the Conscious, allowed to describe **what** it is confused about, and a name for it should be negotiated. (Action 2 – Vivify Specific, see page 38)

3. **Complete Action 9: Changing Chairs Introject Action**, see page 99.

4. **Complete Action 12: Imagery Check**, see page 61.

4.1.3 Action 9: The Changing Chairs Introject Action

The Changing Chairs Introject Action helps Resource States to get a better understanding of the dynamic that exists between them and another person. By experiencing sitting in the chair of the other person and returning to their own chair, clients can have a cathartic experience that can help them resolve confusion, guilt, or blame. Clients bring back to their chair the Sensory Experience Memory of the feelings they had as the Introject.

99

The eight steps below were adapted from *Resource States* (2014) and a more detailed description of this Action can be found in that book, along with case illustrations.

1. **Vivify Specific:** Make sure the pathological state is Conscious and named, e.g., 'Hurt'. It is also okay during this process to use the client's name, rather than the name of the Resource State, as the Vaded State will automatically come into the Conscious when the Client begins speaking with the Introject directly.

2. **Determine what needs to be said and/or asked:** Speak directly with the Resource, calling it by name, and find out what it would like to say to the Introject if it had a chance, and what questions it would like to ask.

3. **Create an understanding of the Introject in the other chair:** I.e., "Hurt, just imagine the presence of your brother sitting in the chair opposite you right now. Tell me when you have done this."

4. **Ensure complete expression and questions:** Tell the Resource that since we know the Introject is really not in the other chair now, this is a time that absolutely anything can be said completely and safely, and direct the Resource to express itself fully and **directly** to the Introject. If the client says something like, "I want him to know…" stop him or her and say, "Tell him directly. Say his name then continue with what you want him to know." The Resource can also ask any questions that it may choose or benefit from. The therapist should **encourage complete expression** and should take good notes of everything that is said so later when the Introject is speaking all appropriate cues can be made.

5. **Direct the client to move to the Introject's chair:** After the Resource has been encouraged to fully express, and to fully question, the client should be asked to stand, move over to the other chair, and when the client is in the process of sitting down, the name of the Introject should be called out clearly, e.g.,

   - "Anthony, thank you for being here."
   - When the client has finished sitting down, the Introject should be asked how it feels about what was just said, e.g., "Anthony, she said

a lot of things to you just now. How does that make you feel?" This helps the client settle into the skin of the Introject.

6. **Speak directly with the Introject:** Ask the Introject questions in relation to the needs of the Resource. Ask things that will enlighten the Resource about the abilities, feelings, and level of peace of the Introject. Look at the notes you have taken and make sure the Introject responds to all the comments and questions posed by the Resource.

7. **Direct the client back to the original chair:** Call the client by name (not the name of the Resource), and ask him or her to stand up and move over to the other chair, and as the client is sitting down speak clearly the name of the Resource or the Client in order to re-engage with that personality part, e.g., "Hurt, what Anthony said was interesting. He said…."

8. **Debrief with the Resource:** Ask the Resource its feelings about what it has just heard, and see if it has anything else it wants to say to the Introject. Debrief.

4.1.4   Importance of SEMs in this Action

One of the most powerful uses of SEMs in therapy is their use to enable states to resolve confusion by internalizing the Sensory Experience Memory of having just spoken as another person. When a client takes on the Introject of the person central to the confusion, then returns to the clients chair the client brings back a SEM of the internalized feelings of the other person. It is the immediate return to the state that had carried a feeling of confusion, when the SEM is still fresh, that facilitates the cathartic breakthrough and understanding that is desired.

For example, a client who may have been frustrated by mother's inability to change can gain a deeper level of understanding. While sitting in mother's chair, being mother, and talking as mother, the client is able to feel the frailties of mother, the anxieties of mother, and then when the client returns to her own chair the client brings back the feelings 'of mother'. This helps the client to better emotionally understand the dynamic and helps the client to feel less confused.

4.1.5   Loss and Grief

Beginnings and endings are special things. Births and deaths bring a reality to the meaning of life. People who have witnessed these often gain a greater appreciation for the time that is spent here.

There's a natural process in grieving, whether it is grieving the loss of a loved one, or grieving some other type of loss. Grieving can appropriately be a bittersweet experience, bitter because of the sadness and sweet because of the memory of the love. Sadness can be a reflection of love. The loving parent can feel sad when their child is hurt.

Clients who present in therapy with grieving as an issue may merely need education, or they may be suffering from a type of complicated bereavement. It is good to understand what is normal in grieving, and what is associated with complicated bereavement.

It is normal, when a person suffers loss, for that person to experience a deep sadness. This type of sadness is not a heavy, negative feeling. It is a reflection of the love or appreciation that was felt. It is normal to miss the person, or what was lost. It is normal to reflect in a wistful way. It is normal to cry. Some people cry without tears. It is normal to feel out of control in terms of when happiness may be felt or in terms of when tears may come. It is normal to continue to feel a connection, or a presence, and it is also normal not to. It is normal in the first few days of grieving to feel confusion, anger, regret, or blame.

These feelings of confusion, anger, regret, or blame are heavy feelings. They relate to something negative. Where sadness is, "Something I love is not here," heavier feelings connect with, "Someone did something wrong."

It is these heavier feelings that relate to complicated bereavement. If a client presents having experienced these heavier feelings for an extended period of time, a therapeutic intervention is important. There is no need for the natural process of grieving to be chronically interrupted by negative, heavy feelings. A Resource State Vaded with Confusion most often results with these feelings.

Clients who present with grieving as their issue will normally either have a Resource State Vaded with Confusion or a Resource State Vaded with Disappointment.

A Resource State Vaded with Disappointment is connected to depression. The person with the Resource State Vaded with Disappointment will exhibit a lower level of energy and will refuse to reengage in many aspects of living. If the client exhibits these symptoms then the therapeutic procedures should be followed for a Resource State Vaded with Disappointment.

More common for a client presenting with grief as an issue is a Resource Vaded with Confusion. This person will be able to participate normally in many aspects of living, but will be unable to let go of a deep level of confusion surrounding their loss. While clients should not be encouraged to "let go" of something loved, clients should also not have to experience a negative rumination surrounding the loss.

A client with a Resource State Vaded with Confusion will report, "I just can't stop thinking about it." They will report things like, "I just wish I had said…, I just can't understand why…, or, I just can't get over this anger."

The process of assisting someone to let go of rumination is not the same thing as assisting someone to let go of the love or appreciation that was felt. By letting go of negative and heavy emotions, clients will be able to better connect with the love and appreciation that they have.

In order to assist a client in letting go of the confusion around a loss, straightforward RT Actions can be used for working with Resource States Vaded with Confusion. The core action in helping the client let go of confusion is the Changing Chairs Introject Action.

It will be important for the client working with grief to speak with the Introject that any negative feelings relate to. For example, the client may speak with the Introject of their deceased loved one, express to that person any feelings and regrets that are held, then change to the chair of the deceased loved one. While in the chair of the deceased loved one the client will have an opportunity to respond from that Introject. Then, when returning to their own chair the client's level of confusion will have changed.

The feelings that are experienced in the chair of the Introject are brought back to the client, and this can provide a cathartic experience of relief and understanding. It is interesting that talking directly with a client for weeks cannot bring the same emotional relief as the Changing Chairs Introject Action can provide in one session.

When working with grief, clients may be asked to speak to the Introject of a pet, of God, to a person with whom they are angry, or to any other Introject that is involved in the negative feelings. It is important for them, when in the Introject's chair, to be encouraged to speak as if they are the Introject, as a great actor would. In other words, it is important for them to emotionally respond as the Introject.

This RT Action can result in the dispelling of confusion, while, when desired, maintaining a loving connection.

It is always important to relate empathetically with clients who present with grieving as an issue. They will vary greatly in regards to their level of grief, and in regards to what they have lost. A client may have lost a loved one, a pet, their health, a relationship, their youth, or any of a large number of other things that they have appreciated. The common factor in grieving is that there was something of importance that has been lost.

4.1.6 Heavy Emotions

Heavy emotions are pathological. They include blame, anger, guilt, hate, shame, and generally, any guilt or blame emotions. They are what I call, 'Someone did something wrong' emotions. That someone can be the client or someone who the client is tied to.

When the negative emotions are directed toward another person they are binding. To blame someone is to hang onto an association with that person. It is impossible to let something go, to allow a person or their act to be history, if blame continues to create a bind with that person. The most powerful way to disempower a negative act is to release the feelings toward the person who committed that act. To continue to blame is to continue to empower the negative act. To say, "I am letting go of that blame," is to disempower the negativity the negative act had created. It is often impossible to let something go if there is confusion about it, i.e., "How could they have done that?" That confusion can be dispelled with the Changing Chairs Introject Action.

> **Key** Sadness is not a heavy emotion. It is a reflection of love. It is part of a normal grieving process. It is what a parent may feel about a difficulty their child is having. Sorrow is part of normal living, but blame, guilt, or hate are binding, dark or heavy emotions. These are unneeded. It is appropriate for clients to be able to grieve with sadness.

4.2 Skills for Day 4

Practice: Vaded with Confusion: You should practice this technique to make sure you are able to work with a state that is Vaded with Confusion. Before you do the practice, look at each step carefully to make sure you understand the purpose of every step. This will help you feel more ready when you practice.

4.2.1 Action 9 Changing Chairs Introject Action

1. Vivify Specific to the Confused State:
2. Ask what needs to be said and/or asked:
3. Create an understanding of the Introject in the other chair:
4. Ensure complete expression and questions:
5. Direct the client to move to the Introject's chair: the Introject should be asked how it feels
6. Speak directly with the Introject:
7. Direct the client back to the original chair:

8. Debrief

For video examples go to www.tinyurl.com/learnresourcetherapy.

4.3 Quiz and Activity for Day 4 Training

4.3.1 Quiz

1. During resolution, is it important that a perpetrator be able to express using, Introject Speak?

2. What is the one word that best describes how a state Vaded with Confusion exhibits?

3. What is SEM?

4. How does SEM help a client gain a better understanding when using the Changing Chairs Introject Action?

5. What type of pathological state is evident when a client is depressed?

6. When should the name of the Introject be first called out when using the Changing Chairs Action, by the therapist?

7. Why is it better to instruct a client to change chairs, rather than ask for their permission?

8. What should be done if the client does not speak directly to the Introject in the empty chair?

9. Why is it important to call out the Introject's name, and ask the Introject how he or she feels about what has just been said?

10. When are states most normally Vaded with Confusion?

4.3.2 Activity

Describe in detail what occurs during each of the following steps.

1. Vivify Specific to the Confused State:

2. Ask what needs to be said and/or asked:

3. Create an understanding of the Introject in the other chair:

4. Ensure complete expression and questions:

5. Direct the client to move to the Introject's chair: the Introject should be asked how it feels

6. Speak directly with the Introject:

7. Direct the client back to the original chair:

8. Debrief

5 Day 5 States Vaded with Fear or Rejection

The emphasis of Day 5 is to learn to help clients who have states that have taken on childhood trauma. These states are responsible for most unwanted emotions and anxieties. When they come into the conscious they bring their unresolved feelings with them.

States Vaded with Fear or Rejection are core to many psychological disorders, plus they are core to all psychological addictions. Today's training is necessary before the Day 6 training in Retro Avoiding states (states that cause addictions), because it is necessary to learn how to resolve the vaded states that the Retro States are avoiding. Resolving states Vaded with Fear or Rejection is the first step in stopping addictions.

A short definition of the day five terms is provided below. You should make sure you are comfortable with the fuller meaning of these terms by the end of this day's training.

5.1 Core Concepts for Day 5 Training

Page #'s are Hyperlinks on eBooks.		Page
Panic Disorder	Panic Disorder is caused when a state Vaded with a high level of Fear comes to the Conscious. The SEM and the Intellectual Memory are often disconnected with Panic Disorder.	110

Anorexia and Bulimia	Both of these result from a state Vaded with Rejection. The Anorexic seeks connection through weight loss, and the Bulimic competes for approval.	112
Sexual and other Abuse	Most often manifests in states Vaded with Fear and anxiety. These Vaded States need empowerment.	115
Working with a State Vaded with Fear	This state must be Conscious to both locate the ISE and during work for it to gain empowerment.	117
Working with a State Vaded with Rejection	This state needs to learn, while Conscious, that it is lovable.	120

5.1.1 Panic Disorder

Panic Disorder and PTSD are caused by states Vaded with Fear. A Resource State has experienced something extremely scary, often interpreted as life-threatening, and then that Resource State has not received any appropriate crisis intervention following the event. When this occurs this Resource State will hang onto the negative feelings, will interpret them as still happening, and when that Resource State comes to the Conscious it will bring with it the same panic it experienced during the initial sensitizing event.

When bridging occurs, taking the client back to the initial sensitizing event, the therapist is able to interact with the Vaded State as it felt at that time. It will be expressing the same feelings that it experiences during a panic attack. A panic attack during a therapy session is referred to as an abreaction. Clients who abreact during a session reveal that they are experiencing the unresolved emotions of a Resource State Vaded with Fear.

Unless the therapist is capable of working with a Resource State that is frightened and upset, bridging should not be undertaken. If the therapist bridges a client suffering from panic attack or PTSD to an initial sensitizing event and then immediately attempts to get the client to relax and feel better, a re-traumatizing will have occurred. In other words taking a client to a traumatic event and then backing out, and doing nothing, only brings the client closer to those traumatized feelings. But, if the client is taken to an initial sensitizing event and the Vaded State is helped to understand, while it is Conscious

- that the Introjects within that event no longer exist,
- that it is now safe,
- that it can say anything it wants to say safely, and
- that it can have additional safety and support from other stronger mature Resource States,

then de-traumatizing has occurred. The previously Vaded State is no longer Vaded, as it has returned to a Normal Condition, with feelings of safety and support. It can even return to its original role, whether that was play or something else. If it was play, the client most often will report finding an additional ability to enjoy playful moments in life.

The one thing that is most important in ensuring that the State Vaded with Fear moves to a Normal Condition is to ensure that the Vaded State is in the Conscious during the intervention process. The Vaded State will not receive a resolution if the therapist is talking with an intellectual state. As soon as a name is received for the Vaded State it should continue to be called by that name and all questions should relate to its experiences and feelings. Intellectual questions such as, "Why," or "What do you think of this" should be avoided. Questions such as these take the client away from the Vaded State and into an intellectual state.

When the state that has carried the fearful feelings receives the intervention while Conscious (Actions 4 to 7), then it is no longer Vaded. It is in a normal condition.

The process of moving a State Vaded with Fear to a state of normality can happen very quickly. Afterwards, clients will show immediate change and this change is permanent. There is an obvious difference in the feelings of the state once RT Actions 4 through 7 have been completed.

5.1.2   Anorexia and Bulimia

Anorexia Nervosa

Anorexia Nervosa appears to be almost exclusively associated with Vaded States that have had initial sensitizing events of rejection. The child has felt unable to have an unconditionally accepting relationship with a parental figure. This does not mean that such a relationship was not offered. It does mean it was not interpreted as unconditionally loving by the child.

The child becomes extremely needy for clear emotional connection, and is finally able to achieve that connection through the demonstration of real concern that is exhibited when the child stops eating. This subconscious dynamic is very difficult to break, as the need for a loving connection is being fulfilled by the parent's attempts to keep the child safe and healthy. The child who has experienced, over time, an unconditional acceptance, becomes more resilient to incidents that could be interpreted as rejection.

When the client suffering from Anorexia Nervosa, during therapy, assumes the Introject of their strongest parental figure, they reveal a difficulty to share unconditional love. For example, if Annette is the client who suffers from Anorexia Nervosa, and she is asked to sit in the opposite chair and assume the identity of her mother, when she, as her mother, speaks back to Annette she will have difficulty showing unconditional love. This parent will most often be highly complementary of success, and will be good at helping the child become successful, but approval tends to become associated with achievement.

The parental Introject is the child's internalized impression of the parent, and does not necessarily reflect the real parent. It is the Introject that is directly connected to the feelings of the client. The parental Introject of the client suffering Anorexia Nervosa, at these times, will say things like:

Therapist: (After hearing from the Introject that she loves her daughter) Just tell her that you love her now. Tell her out loud so I can hear you.

112

Parent: She knows I love her.

Therapist: Just tell her now.

Parent: Well, she knows that.

Therapist: I want to hear you say it. Just tell her that you love her.

Parent speaking in an insincere and matter-of-fact fashion: "Well, of course I love you."

This statement, spoken like this, does not come across as sincere and is not heard as unconditional love. The experience of clients suffering from Anorexia Nervosa is that, no matter what they do, it is not good enough to get unconditional acceptance. They have attempted, sometimes for years, to receive, and feel unconditional love. Then, they discover that by controlling the amount they eat they can get real concern from the parent whose love they have felt deprived of. They discover that, by controlling what they eat, they can see concern and loving emotion for possibly the first time in their lives.

While they have a Resource that is Vaded with Rejection, a 'Helping Resource' (a Retro Avoiding State) learns on the subconscious level that the expression of love that has been needed can be received by losing weight. The more weight they lose the greater the expression of concern they receive. This coping mechanism to receive sincere emotion is not intellectually understood by the client. The client merely feels out of control, and has a powerful driving force to be thin.

Clients can become creative in ways they achieve thinness. They can use many different techniques for this, or combinations of techniques, that include under eating, over exercise, laxatives, and Bulimia.

As long as the client has a Resource Vaded with Rejection that client can maintain issues with food, even in older adulthood. The Vaded Resource needs to be brought to the Conscious, needs to understand through the experience of taking on the persona of the introjected parent, that the problem is the parent's inability to express love, not that the child is unlovable.

This Resource needs to understand that, as does every child, it deserves unconditional love no matter what it does. It needs to experience this unconditional love in the 'Relief' phase of resolution (Action 7, page 54). Many clients with anorexia nervosa have difficulty finding an unconditionally nurturing part of themselves to offer love to the Vaded State. This can slow therapy, as this part often needs practice becoming more nurturing.

A further difficulty in helping an anorexic child is that, as part of the therapy, the child will most often become less frantic to achieve perfection, as the Vaded State begins to feel better about itself. It is common for the dominant parent to fight against this in an attempt to help the child excel. This can slow progress. It appears that this dominant parent may have a state Vaded with Rejection creating a pathological need for their child to excel. This parent rarely wants to become a client in therapy.

It is best if the parent and child can both gain resolution for their Vaded States at the same time (in separate therapy sessions). It is beneficial to the child if the parent learns to give unconditional love, non-related to performance. A good illustration of the change needed in the anorexic's parent is the change in Harrison Ford in the movie, Regarding Henry.

When the Vaded State can gain this understanding, that it is lovable, and when it can gain an experience of being loved, it will feel comfortable remaining as an underlying state, continuing to gain love and acceptance from a nurturing part of the personality. This resolution of the Vaded State with Rejection, bringing it into a Normal Resource Condition, allows the mature Resources of the client to make decisions that are healthy and empowered.

Bulimia Nervosa

While a client that has Anorexia Nervosa may use Bulimia to achieve weight loss, often individuals may become Bulimic completely independent of Anorexia Nervosa. Bulimia can be a way that clients with Resources Vaded with Rejection can compete with others in their desire to gain love.

Because individuals who have Resources Vaded with Rejection have a tendency to compare themselves with others, they often have concerns about their body image. Their concern about not being lovable enough can translate to high anxiety if they feel other people have an advantage over them. They can be driven to be 'just as good' or 'better' than others. When they see others with bodies they think are better than theirs they can become highly motivated to lose weight.

It is not unusual for a person who has never been Bulimic to learn bulimic behavior from others and take up the practice. Of course, bulimic behavior is very hard on the body. It can be injurious to organs, the stomach acid can destroy the teeth; it can shorten life, and even kill.

When the Bulimic individual gets a resolution to the Vaded State with Rejection that person will no longer be driven by high anxiety to compete. He or she will still be able to make reasoned decisions on eating and lifestyle, but those decisions will be within the control of the individual.

Clients who suffer from Bulimia that is not associated with Anorexia will often respond quickly to the therapeutic intervention for States Vaded with Rejection. When Bridging leads to the correct ISE and the associated Vaded State is resolved, a positive outcome can be expected.

The difference between having a Vaded State and having a Normal State is the ability to be empowered and have control in life. Often, the person who feels like they have low control is actually very controlling. They constantly attempt to control things because they have a Resource that feels out of control. That Resource will remain out-of-control until it receives resolution, then the individual will be able to actually be in control, and feel in control of their own life. That person will no longer have to fight for control. He or she will be able to use reason and assertive Resources to make decisions and carry them through.

5.1.3   Sexual and other Abuse

Most clients who have suffered abuse have Resource States Vaded with Fear. It is not unusual for them also to have Resource States Vaded with Rejection.

An important aspect about working with the client who has suffered abuse is to refrain from assuming that the presented issue is directly associated with that abuse. Too often both clients and therapists assume that issues relate to abuse, even when they do not. Of course, many issues do relate to abuse, but the bridging techniques in RT Action 3, Bridging, will be able to locate the initial sensitizing event that relates to changes the client is interested in making.

All clients have issues, not only clients who have suffered abuse. There is no need to revisit negative times in the lives of clients unless doing so results in resolving the issues that clients are ready to change.

When bridging takes a client to an initial sensitizing event involving abuse the client does not need to go into any detail about that abuse. Resolution has to do with empowerment. It does not have to do with regurgitating details. RT is not a voyeuristic therapy. What is important is that the state that sees the Introject of an abuser as powerful, learns that that Introject has no power within the personality. It is important for the Resource State that felt disempowered to learn that it can now have its space where it is in control, safe, supported and loved.

The client does not have to go into any detail about anything that has happened. It is important for the state that was Vaded with Fear to be able to express fully to the abuser, and that state is better enabled to do this with the help of the therapist. The therapist can say things like, "Let's just shrink him down to 1 inch tall," or, "Is it okay if I talk to him first?"

It is important for the state that was Vaded with Fear to be able to express fully to the abuser so that it can realize there is now nothing inside that can hurt it. It realizes this by experiencing that it can say absolutely anything completely freely. When it realizes this, then it has the power to ask the abuser to leave its inner space. Therefore, a Resource State that had been Vaded, can become empowered, can gain a feeling of safety, and with RT Action 4, Relief, it can feel supported and loved. It can be left in a bright, loving space, no longer hanging on to fears from the past.

This kind of intervention does not change the past, it changes the emotions the person continues to carry from the past. Revisiting a negative memory will always be difficult, but when the client no longer carries the seething emotions of fear and rejection from the past, that client will be able to respond to current challenges with mature Resource States that can best deal with them.

The client who presents with a State Vaded with Fear will be able to discover with the therapist if that state was Vaded during abuse or during any other time. The next section provides the steps to follow to work with Resource States Vaded with Fear.

5.1.4   Working with a State Vaded with Fear

The following Actions move a state from a Vaded with Fear condition to a Normal Condition. The state Vaded with Fear carries a belief that an Introject can harm it. It believes that something on the inside has power. This is an illusion. It is fearing a memory fragment. These steps insure that the state that needs change is Conscious and that this Vaded State learns it has more power than the Introject. At the end of the process the state that had been carrying fear feels empowered, safe, and supported.

From Vaded with Fear to Normal Condition

1. (Action 1: Diagnosis) The correct state must be identified by the therapist as the core cause of the presenting concern. See page 73
2. (Action 2: Vivify Specific) Ensure that the Vaded State is truly in the Conscious to the needed level. See page 38
3. (Action 3: Bridging) Bridging must take the Vaded State to the image of the original sensitizing event. See page 39
4. (Action 4: Expression) Ensure the Resource expresses its feelings fully. See page 51
5. (Action 6: Removal) Give the Resource a choice to keep or remove the **Introjects** that gave it negative feelings. See page 54
6. (Action 7: Relief) Bring a nurturing, caring Resource of the client to the fragile state to ensure that it gets support and care. See page 54
7. (Action 8: Find Resource) If needed, find the best Resource for the client to handle this situation in the future. See page 56
8. (Action 12: Imagery Check) Go back to the image from Action 2: Vivify Specific to ensure the desired change has been achieved. See page 61.

Using RT Action 2, Vivify Specific

One of the most important aspects of treating a client who has a State Vaded with Fear is to first make sure that the Vaded State is Conscious. This means that RT Action 2, Vivify Specific, must be used in order to bring out a specific time this Vaded State has been conscious.

If the Vaded State is a Vaded Conscious State (see page 34) this process is not difficult. The client will present with the issue being the negative emotions that are experienced when this Vaded State is conscious. Therefore, the therapist merely needs to vivify a precise time that the state was conscious using RT Action 2.

If the Vaded State is a Vaded Avoided State (see page 34) the process is a bit more complex. The Vaded State may have only been out for a moment prior to a Retro Avoiding State taking over the Conscious in order to save the personality from the negative feelings of the Vaded State. This means that the therapist needs to use imagery to find the precise time the client decided to use the Retro Avoiding Behavior. Imagery may be used to assist the client to imagine delaying the Retro Avoiding Behavior. When this is done properly the anxiety of the client will increase, and this increase in anxiety is the Vaded Avoided State coming into the Conscious. At this point Bridging may occur. Transcribed case examples of this dialog are available in *Resource Therapy* (Emmerson, 2014).

Using RT Action 3, Bridging

When Bridging to a State Vaded with Fear, the client will sometimes become quite emotional. If the therapist is not willing to work with a client exhibiting high levels of emotion, Bridging should not be used. It can be re-traumatizing to bridge the client to a traumatic initial sensitizing event, if no therapeutic intervention follows. The positive thing is, it is de-traumatizing to bridge the client to a traumatic event and then resolve that trauma using the Expression, Removal and Relief Actions.

Some therapists are not comfortable with clients who show anxiety. These therapists will sometimes attempt to move the client immediately away from the anxiety by relaxing them and giving them positive images to help them feel better. They may call this ego strengthening. This is precisely the wrong thing to do when working with Vaded States. When the client is moved away from anxiety the client is moved away from the state that needs resolution. It is imperative that the state that needs resolution gain the empowerment and support that it needs. It cannot do this unless it is in the Conscious.

Clients with States Vaded with Fear will demonstrate different levels of emotion following Bridging. Regardless of the level of emotion, it is important for the therapist to move directly to the Expression, Removal, and Relief resolution Actions as soon as the initial sensitizing event has been located.

Using RT Action 4, Expression

Whether the client fears the Introject of another person, the Introject of an animal, or the Introject of something like a fire, a flood, or a storm, Expression to what has been feared is empowering. The therapist should make it easy for the client to express to what was feared so the client will be able to understand there is nothing currently internal that is harmful.

The therapist may make it easy to express by suggesting that the feared Introject be shrunk, or the therapist may speak to the feared Introject first. Regardless of what the therapist does to help this happen, it is important that the Conscious Vaded State speak directly to the Introject it has feared, because this is a step that allows it to understand it can say absolutely anything safely. It learns by speaking freely that there is nothing internal that can hurt it.

Using RT Action 6, Removal

Following Expression, the Resource State is given the opportunity to decide whether it wants its Introject to stay in its inner space, or leave. It does not matter how this decision is made. Having the power to make this decision is empowering.

Using RT Action 7, Relief

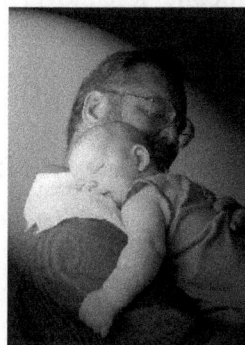

An important step in resolving a State Vaded with Fear is to find a nurturing, internal Resource State that can stay with it and give support to the previously Vaded State. As explained in the Relief Actions section (page 54), it is important to find a state that wants to do this.

At the end of the Relief Action, it is good to ask the previously Vaded State if it would like a new name. A state that may have previously been named 'Frightened 'may choose a new name, such as, 'Safe'. It can be asked to choose a name that fits how it feels currently.

Using RT Action 8, Find Resource

A State Vaded with Fear may have prevented the preferred Resource State from taking on an activity. A childhood State Vaded with Fear may have prevented a communicative state from being able to talk in front of a group. Following the resolution of the State Vaded with Fear it can be helpful to use the Find Resource Action to find a more appropriate state for the activity. For example, a state that enjoys communicating can be found to help the client enjoy communicating to groups, following the resolution of a Vaded State that held a fear of judgement.

Using RT Action 12, Imagery Check

The original image from RT Action 2 can be used in the Imagery Check to ensure that the client no longer experiences the unwanted emotional reaction. See Imagery Check, page 61

5.1.5   Working with a State Vaded with Rejection

The following Actions move a state from a Vaded with Rejection pathological Condition to a non-pathological Normal Condition. The state Vaded with Rejection carries a belief that it is unlovable or not good enough. This is an illusion. The following steps ensure that the state that needs change is Conscious and that this Vaded State learns it was the Introject that was unable to share unconditional love, not the state that it was unlovable. At the end of the process the state that had been carrying feelings of not being good enough feels nurtured, safe, and loved.

From Vaded with Rejection to a Normal Condition

1. (Action 1: Diagnosis) The correct state must be identified by the therapist as the core cause of the presenting concern. See page 73
2. (Action 2: Vivify Specific) Ensure that the Vaded State is truly in the Conscious to the needed level. See page 38
3. (Action 3: Bridging) Bridging must take the Vaded State to the image of the original sensitizing event. See page 39
4. (Action 4: Expression) Ensure the Resource expresses its feelings fully. See page 51

5. (Action 5: Introject Speak) Allow the Vaded State to speak as the rejecting Introject so it can better understand the inability for the Introject to share love. See page 52

6. (Action 6: Removal) Give the Resource a choice to keep or remove the **Introjects** that gave it negative feelings. See page 54

7. (Action 7: Relief) Bring in a nurturing, caring Resource of the client to the fragile state to ensure that it gets support and care. See page 54

8. (Action 8: Find Resource) If needed, find the best Resource for the client to handle this situation in the future. See page 56

9. (Action 12: Imagery Check) Go back to the image from Action 2: Vivify Specific to ensure the desired change has been achieved. See page 61

Using RT Action 2, Vivify Specific

A State Vaded with Rejection will feel unlovable or incompetent. If a client presents with this as the issue they are ready to change, use the Vivify Specific Action to ensure that the Resource State with this undesired feeling is in the Conscious.

Using RT Action 3, Bridging

When Bridging to a State Vaded with Rejection the client will go to an ISE where a state was unable to feel an unconditional acceptance.

- Sometimes a state feels neglected, or unnoticed by a parent,

- Sometimes the ISE will be at a time when one parent is leaving the household following a relationship separation, and

- Sometimes the ISE will be at a time when a younger sibling is seen as getting more love.

These states have in common Introjects of a parent or Guardian that has not revealed to them unconditional love. This does not mean that the memory of the client is accurate, but it does mean that the Vaded State feels to some degree, unlovable.

Using RT Action 4, Expression

Expression is an important step when there is a Resource State Vaded with Rejection. It is important for the state to be able to say, directly to the protagonist, how that person's action causes it to feel. The client may be encouraged to say things like, "I need you. Why are you leaving?" If the state indicates that they were spoken to in an inappropriate manner, it may be encouraged to say something like, "You have no right to speak to me like that. The way you are speaking to me is wrong."

Statements such as these empower the Resource State Vaded with Rejection. They enable the Resource State to understand that they have the power to say anything that they want.

Using RT Action 5, Introject Speak

When a Resource State has been Vaded with Rejection it is important for it to be able to hear directly from the other person. Following Expression, the therapist can say something like,

- "That was very good. Right now I want to hear directly from Dad. I want you to be like a great actor, forget who you are, so I can hear directly from Dad. You can speak as him now. Dad, your daughter said a lot of things to you right now. How does that make you feel, Dad?"

Because the Resource State feels rejection from the Introject, the Introject will always respond in a less than unconditionally loving manner. This reflects the internalized impression the Resource State has of the Introject.

The Introject may say things like, "Of course I love her. I work all day because of her." But, when asked to express that love back to the Vaded State the Introject will say things like, "Well, she knows I love her." Introjects will sometimes say things like, "She is very demanding. I have too many things to do. I should not have had kids."

There should be no attempt to change an Introject. This would seem inauthentic to the client. It is okay if a client has an understanding that a parent was not unconditionally loving. That understanding does not have to be changed. What needs to be changed is the experience of the child feeling unlovable.

Therefore, after Introject Speak it is a very important step to return and speak directly with the Vaded State and say something like,

- "I can really understand why you feel the way you do now. Your 'Dad' is not very good at showing unconditional love. Every child deserves unconditional love, no matter what. Even when they make mistakes, every child deserves unconditional love. I want to make sure you get the love that every child deserves."

Statements like these change the experience from, "I am unlovable," to, "I did not receive the love that every child deserves." There is no attempt to make the Introject a villain. Statements can be made like, "I'm sorry at this point in his life your dad was not able to show unconditional love. Hopefully, later he can get better at doing that."

Using RT Action 6, Removal

The Removal Action is the same as it was for working with Resource States Vaded with Fear. The state is merely asked whether or not it prefers the other person to remain in its inner space. It does not matter how this question is answered. It is the power that it perceives in being able to answer the question that is important. For example,

- "I want to make sure you get the love you deserve, in the meantime do you want your dad in this space where you are right now on the inside, or do you want a clear space? You can have it any way you want, and it will not affect what your adult parts do."

If the state says, "I don't want him here," or, "He can leave," I just say, "That's fine. Just tell him he can go now." The fact that the previously Vaded State has been able to say absolutely anything and still be okay gives it the power to have its inner space the way it prefers.

If the state says, "No, he can stay," I just say, "That's nice. Just let him know he can stay."

Using RT Action 7, Relief

This is where a helping Resource State is brought in to assist the previously Vaded State. See RT Action 7, page 54, for instructions. At the conclusion of this Action the client should feel safe, supported and loved. If a negative sounding name had been given to the Resource State, at this point it is good to ask the state what name would better fit the way it feels now. Clients will sometimes report that when the state was able to change its name to reflect its new feelings the change somehow felt institutionalized.

Using RT Action 8, Find Resource

Following the resolution of the Vaded State, that state will be in a Normal Condition. States Vaded with Rejection are almost always childhood states, therefore it is unlikely that it will be the best state, the most preferred state, for the client to handle the situation described in RT Action 2.

RT Action 8, Find Resource (see page 56) can be used to ensure that the client will have the most preferred Resource in the Conscious for those times in the future.

Using RT Action 12, Imagery Check

The final Action, once preferred resources have been found to deal with a situation in the future, is to do and Imagery Check in order to allow the client to experience the imagery of the original presentation with the new and preferred Resource in the Conscious (See Imagery Check, page 61).

5.2   Skills for Day 5

Practice: Working with a State Vaded with Rejection or Fear

> It is very important to become comfortable working with states Vaded with Fear or Rejection. More clients present with states Vaded with Rejection than with any other issue. Before you do the practice, look at each step carefully to make sure you understand the purpose of every step. This will help you feel more ready when you practice. For video examples go to www.tinyurl.com/learnresourcetherapy.

5.2.1 Resolving States Vaded with Fear or Rejection

1. Isolate issue

2. Vivify Specific

3. Bridge

4. Expression, (Introject Speak if state is vaded with Rejection)

5. Removal

6. Relief

7. Find Resource

8. Imagery Check

5.3 Quiz and Activities for Day 5 Training

5.3.1 Quiz

1. What type of pathological Resource State causes panic disorder?

2. What type of pathological Resource State is associated with low self-esteem?

3. When working with an ISE relating to sexual abuse, is it important that detail be obtained?

4. Why should therapists not assume that a pathological issue is necessarily related to sexual abuse?

5. What if bridging takes the client to an issue other than sexual abuse when the client thought their problem was because of sexual abuse?

6. What type of pathological Resource State is associated with anorexia?

7. What type of pathological Resource State is associated with bulimia?

8. What benefit does an anorexic client gain from losing weight?

9. Why should the Introject of the rejecting parent be spoken with by the therapist when revisiting the ISE?

10. What comment should be made to the Vaded State after speaking with the Introject of a rejecting parent?

5.3.2   Activity

Write a list of 5 things a client might present with who has a State Vaded with Fear.

1. _____
2. _____
3. _____
4. _____
5. _____

See Resources Vaded with Fear can cause these Pathologies

Write a list of 5 things a client might present with who has a State Vaded with Rejection.

1. _____
2. _____
3. _____
4. _____
5. _____

See Resources Vaded with Rejection can cause these Pathologies

6 Day 6 Retro States & Vaded with Disappointment

This is a big training day. It combines the training of working with states Vaded with Fear or Rejection with Retro State Negotiation. Retro States are strong and, while Conscious, they are in full control.

It is important to get a good understanding of Action 10: Retro State Negotiation in order to help clients cease unwanted behavior. These are very powerful techniques when applied correctly, so it is worth taking the time to get a good understanding of Retro States and what they are doing.

Retro State Negotiation is also used when working with a State Vaded with Disappointment, therefore learning to help depressed clients is also covered in Day 6 training. Both Retro States and States Vaded with Disappointment overpower other states. It is most important to work with them, rather than against them.

A short definition of the day six terms is provided below. You should make sure you are comfortable with the fuller meaning of these terms by the end of this day's training.

6.1 Core Concepts for Day 6 Training

Page #'s are Hyperlinks on eBooks.		Page
Diagnosis of Retro States	A Retro State it does a behavior another state does not like.	128

6.1 Core Concepts for Day 6 Training		
Retro Original vs Retro Avoiding	Retro Original behavior started when the state was formed, while Retro Avoiding behavior is learned to avoid the bad feelings of a state Vaded with Fear or Rejection.	130
Action 10 Retro State Negotiation	This is negotiation that enables a Retro State to fulfil its purpose with preferred behavior rather than with unwanted behavior.	130
Addictions	Retro Avoiding behavior. This is behavior beyond the control of the client.	132
Anger/Rage issues	Anger is normally Retro Avoiding while Rage is normally Retro Original. Vaded States feel weak, while Retro States feel strong.	136
Working with Depression	A combination of Finding Resources and Retro State Negotiation.	139
Keeping purpose and trading purviews	A part of Action 10 where the Retro State is praised for its purpose and where it learns to continue to accomplish its purpose using a more preferred behavior.	144

6.1.1   Diagnosis of Retro States

The main thing to remember in identifying Retro States is a Retro State conducts a behavior that another state does not like. When the client says, "I wish I did not do that," or "I hate myself when I am like that," there is a Retro State conducting behavior that another state does not like. The table below reviews Retro States in relation to the other pathologies.

Table 16 The Eight Types of State Pathologies

Vaded with Fear	**All Vaded States exhibit emotions** that are problematic to the client.
Vaded with Rejection	
Vaded with Disappointment	
Vaded with Confusion	
Retro Original	**All Retro States exhibit behaviors** that are problematic to the client.
Retro Avoiding	
Conflicted	**Inner Conflict** that is problematic.
Dissonant	**Not the best** state out.

Whenever the client is complaining about his or her own behavior, not feelings, a Retro State is responsible. Retro states are powerful states that believe what they do is important. They are used to being not liked, and they often think they will never be. A Retro State will often only agree to take on new behavior after learning it can be liked by other states. When a state that never thought it could be liked is able to feel being liked, and when it knows it can continue to accomplish its mission and be liked at the same time, it becomes ready to change.

6.1.2   Retro Original vs Retro Avoiding

Retro Original behavior is behavior that was learned in childhood when the Resource State was forming as a coping skill. It became Retro when another state became unhappy with its behavior. Examples include rage, pouting, passive aggressive behavior, and many personality disorders.

Retro Avoiding behavior is behavior that the client has learned, usually in adulthood, that helps the client avoid the negative feelings of a Vaded State. Examples include addictions, OCD, workaholism, and reactive anger.

All Retro States believe what they do is important. They are strong and have the ability to override other states in order to insure the behavior they believe is important gets done.

6.1.3   Retro State Negotiation

Retro State Negotiation may be carried out immediately with Retro Original States, but prior to using this activity with Retro Avoiding States it is necessary to first resolve the Vaded State that is being avoided.

Retro Avoiding States are those that carry out all avoiding behaviors, such as addictions, OCD, compulsive shopping, and others. A more detailed description of the steps and a case illustration can be found in *Resource Therapy* (Emmerson, 2014).

Here are the steps for Retro State Negotiation

1. **Use the Vivify Specific Action** (# 2) to bring the Retro State into the Conscious.

2. **Talk with this state to determine how it has helped the client in the past** in order to become clear on its purpose. For example, a state exhibiting anti-social behavior may have protected the person from attack, or an alcohol abusing state may have protected the client from the negative feelings of a Vaded State.

3. **Get a name for the Retro State** that is an indication of its purpose, not its role. For example, don't accept the name Smoker, rather accept a name like Relaxer, or Rebel. Don't accept the name Gambler, rather accept a name like Protector, or Escape. You can suggest a name once the

purpose is clear, and you can ask the state specifically what its purpose is. Allow the Retro State to have input on its name.

4. **Show appreciation for how it has helped in the past**, even if the behavior has been negative. You do not need to praise the behavior, just the efforts to help. Praise the state for having been willing to be disliked by other states so that it could accomplish its important role.

5. **Line up an appropriate resource.** If another Resource is needed to handle the situation that the Retro State has handled in the past, use the Find Resource Action (#8). For example, if assertive behavior is needed rather than rage, anger or withdrawal, you will need to find a resource that can be assertive by using the Find Resource Action. You can do this step even before the Retro State Negotiation starts if you prefer. It is often important to have a state that can become conscious during some of the times when the Retro State had been in the past.

6. Suggest an alternative or smaller role that will allow it to continue to accomplish its purpose, a role that the other Resources can appreciate. At this time do not ask the Retro State if it will take on this new role. Say, "Let's just see what other states will think of you with this new (or less used) role. It is common for Retro States to at first believe they will never be liked, or to believe that what they have done in the past is all they can do. They will say things like, "They will never like me," or, "This is just what I do. I can't do anything else." It is amazing how quickly these attitudes change once they have experienced another state appreciating its new role. You can say things like, "I know it seems like they will never like you, but I bet they will if you take on this new way of helping. Let's just see."

7. **Speak directly with the Resource that has presented the Retro behavior** as an issue. Get a name for it. Suggest to it that it will like the Retro State if it changes, e.g., "You would like Protector if Protector only comes out when the body is in real physical danger, and if an Assertive part handles things at other times. That would be really good to have a strong Protector part if wild dogs were attacking, wouldn't it? Then at other times Assertive could handle things. That would be okay with you,

wouldn't it? Make sure this state says directly to the Retro State that it will like it if it takes on the new role.

8. **Speak again with the Retro State** to ensure it is now willing to take on a new behavior or a reduced role, e.g., "Protector, did you hear that. Other states will like you with your new role. Are you willing to allow Assertive to handle most things while you are there in case the body is ever in real danger?"

6.1.4   Addictions

There are two causes for addictive behavior. These are, 1) psychological causes, and 2) physiological causes. There are addictive behaviors that are caused by a combination of both.

Here, we are interested in the psychological causes of addictions, as well as their interplay with the physiological causes. Often, an addiction will begin due to psychological causes. A physical addiction may develop, and the effort to stop the addiction is complicated by both the physical and psychological causes.

Physical addictions are easy to understand. One can be addicted to drinking coffee, eating sugar, or any other number of drugs. The body becomes accustomed to having a substance and when that substance is withheld the body demands the return of that substance. These addictions can be very difficult to overcome. Personally, if I do not have a cup of coffee by two o'clock in the afternoon I get a headache and flulike symptoms. This is the result of a physiological addiction. I have found, if I want to stop drinking coffee, the best way to do that is to cut my coffee consumption by one third over a period of several days. Without doing this, my body severely demands coffee.

Obviously, if the body's demand for coffee is difficult to overcome, the body's demand for harder drugs can be extremely challenging. Even, those who have been taking antidepressants can attest to the fact that it can be very challenging, physically, to cease taking them.

Psychological addictions are caused by Vaded States. Addictions are actually clever coping mechanisms to avoid the experience of a Vaded State. This is the case, whether it is a drug addiction, gambling addiction, or even workaholism.

A Resource can be vaded with an experience so overwhelming that escaping from that feeling into addictive behavior is easily the lesser of evils. Normally this escape is a subconscious process where a 'helping' Resource has found a way to relieve the psyche from the experience of the Vaded State. For example, the zoning out experience of going into a casino, risking losing money, seeing colorful and flashing lights, can create a relieving diversion from a Vaded State that holds overwhelmingly unpleasant feelings.

Drugs can block states from coming into the Conscious. If an individual has experienced the angst of the Vaded State, then finds a drug that blocks that state from coming into the Conscious, it is very appealing for that person to return to that drug over and over again to receive the peace that it gives. It takes the Vaded State out of the Conscious. When a person finds a drug that helps them in this way, this is called their "Drug of choice."

Some people experiment with drugs without ever becoming addicted. It is likely that these individuals do not have states vaded to a level that creates a need for them to escape. It is even possible for these people to become physically addicted to a drug if they return to it over and over again, purely for recreational purposes.

It is very difficult for the person who is both physically and psychologically addicted to a drug to stop their habit. They have to, at once, deal with the physical addiction and the return of the Vaded State when they stop using the drug. Because of this, it is beneficial for their Vaded States to gain resolution so that all they have to deal with is the physical addiction.

This is tricky, because while the person is under the effects of the drug, the Vaded State that needs resolution is blocked. This means that it is also blocked from a therapeutic resolution, because the therapist has no access to the Vaded State while it is being chemically blocked. In order for the therapist to gain access to this Vaded State that has been blocked by the drug it is necessary for the individual to stop taking the drug long enough for it to reappear.

I instruct my clients who want to cease the use of a drug to stop using that drug for a period of time long enough before their session so they will be yearning for that drug during the session. The number of times they are unable to do this is disheartening, but when they can, they come to the session with the Vaded State associated with their addiction easily accessible.

The only way to remove the psychological need for the drug is to resolve the Vaded State that the drug has blocked. Once the Vaded State is resolved, then the individual will only have to deal with the physiological addiction, if there is one. That can be a difficult task in its own right.

These understandings help us see that drug dependency can be very difficult to break. Clients respond better to therapy when they realize their therapist understands this. They also respond best when the 'helping Resource' that has used a drug to give him relief feels respected. This, drug taking Resource, is most often abused and misunderstood both by other people and by other Resources of the client. It feels that it is important and that unless it does its job, helping the person cope, there will be a lot of pain. The best way to get this personality part on side is to thank it for the help that it has given in the past, and let it know that it is important that it will be available in the future to help the client and other ways.

It is always good to have all Resources cooperating with the therapist. If a Resource believes that it is not respected, or that the therapist is against it, it will likely not cooperate. An important part of helping a client with an addiction is resolving the Vaded State. When that Resource that had previously felt overwhelmingly uncomfortable when coming to the Conscious, finds peace, support and care, there is no longer a need to escape from that state into addictive behavior.

This is the case no matter what kind of an addiction the client presents. It is not unusual for individuals to find an addictive behavior that they can live with that helps them block the experience of a Vaded State. These may include things that on the surface may not appear problematic, like gardening, cooking, cleaning, or workaholism. It is not good when an individual feels compelled to do something, even if it something like gardening. They feel out of control.

134

Some individuals will become so used to having an addiction that they do not want it to end. I suspect many of the most famous people in history were addicted to their work; that is, they could not stop working without their Vaded State returning. Some people like this become proud of their accomplishments and find it difficult to imagine themselves not feeling compelled to work. While excellent work can be accomplished by individuals who are not addicted, it is true that workaholism can result in exceedingly large amounts of hours spent working. The sad part is that these people feel out of control.

People who are addicted to work often find it difficult, or impossible, to take time out, put their feet in the stream, and experience a relaxed moment for any period of time. Quiet moments allow Vaded States to rise to the surface, if they exist. When Vaded States are resolved our moments are our own, to work, to relax, to choose to spend time alone, or with our family or our friends.

What is important for therapists to remember when working with addictions, is that the way to bring resolution to psychological addictions is to bring resolution to the Vaded State that fuels the addiction. To gain access to this state there must be a withdrawal of the addictive behavior so the Vaded State will come to the surface. This means there must be a withdrawal of the drug, if the addiction is a drug addiction, and if the addiction is not a drug addiction there must be a withdrawal of the activity, that prevents the Vaded State from coming into the Conscious. If the addiction is not a drug addiction, this can be done easily with imagery.

Using Vivify Specific, have the client imagine a time immediately prior to beginning the addictive behavior, then have him or her to imagine continuing without starting the addictive behavior. For example, have clients imagine exactly where they are when they feel compelled to go into a casino. Revivify that scene in detail, and have him or her to imagine continuing to stay where they are, without going into the casino. This will bring the Vaded State into the Conscious and Bridging can proceed.

It is important for the therapist to remember that the Retro Avoiding States that have been taking on addictive behavior have been doing this for the benefit of the client, to relieve the client of the overwhelmingly bad feelings of the Vaded State. Therefore, this 'Helping State' needs to be praised, understood, and eventually a new role needs to be found for it so that it can feel it is able to benefit the client without continuing with the addiction. It will be able to do this only when the Vaded State is resolved, and not before.

6.1.5   Anger/Rage issues

There is a difference between anger and rage. Anger can be a normal, healthy emotion, or it can be a defense of a fragile Vaded State, a Retro Avoiding Behavior. Rage is a Retro Original Behavior that is an extension of early childhood tantrum behavior.

Anger

Anger is sometimes a normal emotion that should not be avoided. It should be acknowledged and experienced in a healthy manner. The person operating from Resources in a Normal (healthy) Condition will feel angry, acknowledge the feeling, and respond in a manner that can later be seen as positive.

Anger can also be a Retro Avoiding Behavior. It is not unusual for a person who feels emotionally threatened (a fragile part feels exposed) to lash out in anger. This anger is Retro Avoiding. It is an indication that a Vaded State needs resolution. This anger, Retro Avoiding, state can be thanked during therapy for protecting the fragile state.

A good way to access the Vaded State that has been protected is to ask the state that has demonstrated anger, "What do you feel about that fragile part you have been protecting?" When this question is answered the fragile state can be immediately asked to comment on what was said, e.g., "Fragile part. Anger just said she does not like you very much. That must not feel very good, does it?" When the fragile part gives an answer you can immediately thank it for talking with you and ask it, "What can I call you?"

When the fragile state is in the Conscious you can go ahead and bridge to the ISE and use the Actions 4 to 7 to bring the Vaded state to a Normal Condition. When this state is no longer Vaded the Anger state will no longer have to protect it.

Rage

The client who has rage as an issue has a Retro Original Resource State. The Rage Resource State has almost always developed in childhood. It is important to always talk positively to, and about, all Resources, and the rage Resource State is no exception. The state that rages may have carried out activities that were inappropriate, or even illegal. Still, the client has come to therapy for change and the best way to effect change is to connect positively with all Resource States.

The Rage Resource State can be told that it is good for the person to have such a strong state, that every person could benefit from such a state, and that it is also good to be liked and appreciated by the other parts of the personality. All states like to be liked, even those who say that they don't care.

The key to helping the client who presents with rage is to connect in a positive way directly with the state that exhibits rage, to find an alternative Resource that can be assertive, and to make sure that the client has the ability to determine which state should be conscious at the appropriate time.

The core RT Action that is involved in this process is Retro State Negotiation. The rage state has not felt appreciated in the past. It can be told that it should be appreciated, and that it can be appreciated by all states. It will often at first not believe this.

A suggestion can be made that it is such a powerful state that it only need come out to protect the body from physical danger. A suggestion can be made that during other times it would be more appropriate for an assertive state to come out. This gives the rage state an important role, and in most people's lives the state will never again assume the consciousness.

The rage state may be accessed using the Vivify Specific Action, and an assertive state may be accessed using the Find Resource Action. When a client presents with rage as an issue I often first locate and get a name for a state that can take on assertive behavior prior to speaking with the Resource that takes on rage behavior. That way, when talking with a rage state I can refer to the assertive state with confidence that it will understand what I'm talking about. Here are the steps for working with rage:

1. Use Action 8, to find a Resource that can be Assertive.

2. Use Action 2, to bring into the Conscious the Resource that sometimes Rages.

3. Show appreciation to the Rage Resource and suggest that it only come out when the body is physically in danger, and that at other times the Assertive state can handle the smaller things.

4. Speak with the Resource State that brought the client to therapy and suggest how it would be positive if the rage Resource were available to protect the body when it was in danger, and if the assertive Resource were available to respond to other challenging issues.

5. Make sure that this Resource speaks <u>directly</u> to the Rage Resource, saying that it would appreciate it if it would protect the body from danger, and allow the assertive Resource to respond at other times.

6. Speak again with the rage Resource saying something like, "Did you hear that? You will be liked and appreciated by the other states if you are there to do the very important role of protecting the body. They will all like you and pat you on the back. It is appropriate that they appreciate you because you are an important part of this person."

7. Negotiate with the rage Resource and the assertive Resource making sure that both are pleased with the outcome.

8. Use the Find Resource Action to locate a wise state that can decide which Resource (assertive or rage) is the best Resource at any given time. Make sure this Resource speaks directly with both the rage Resource and the assertive Resource.

9. Use RT Action 12, Imagery Check, to ensure that all Resources understand their agreements.

Following these actions all resources have defined roles, all resources are appreciated, and a wise Resource is left with a responsibility to decide when it is appropriate to be assertive and when it might be appropriate to defend against a pack of wild dogs.

6.1.6   Working with Depression

There are two kinds of depression, organically based depression and psychologically-based depression. Organically based depression can be caused by chemical imbalances, drug use, or physiology. Psychologically-based depression is caused by a profound level of disappointment in the perceived reality. Both types of depression result in physiological changes in the body. The presentation in this text relates to psychologically-based depression, and when the word depression is used it will refer to psychologically-based depression. This is the most common type of depression.

Depression is often misdiagnosed, with a number of clients presenting with the belief that they are depressed when they really have Resource States Vaded with Fear, Rejection, or Confusion. Resource States Vaded with Disappointment relate to depression.

The client suffering from depression will be low in energy, and will have a state with such a profound level of disappointment that it will block other states in their ability to enjoy living. Often, the client will know exactly why he or she is depressed, but sometimes the client is unaware of the reason the disappointed Resource State is blocking other states.

The RT intervention for depression is somewhat similar to the CBT intervention. A CBT therapist will normally encourage the client to begin interacting in life; begin going for walks, and begin taking on more activities. It is not unusual for the depressed client to fail in their attempts to reengage in these activities. The reason for this is the Resource State Vaded with Disappointment will most often continue to block other states from enjoying life, because of its disappointment.

The RT intervention for depression also begins with assisting the client to reengage in living. A difference in the techniques is that the RT therapist speaks directly with the Resource States that have enjoyed activities in the past to ensure that they are willing to take on these activities, and also speaks with the Resource State that is Vaded with Disappointment to gain its permission for these Resource States to begin re-engaging. Therefore, clients more easily and more quickly can begin re-engaging. This is very important.

The depressed client will need time to re-energize before therapy can be completed. Therefore, the sooner Resource States can take on positive activities, the speedier therapy can continue.

No therapy can result in a client who is clinically depressed walking out in the first session in a normal condition. It physiologically takes the body a number of weeks to reengage to a normal level of energy.

The steps and RT Actions for the treatment of States Vaded with Disappointment should be followed to assist clients in their process to return to a normal level of energy. It should be noted that clients who have already begun the use of antidepressants will necessarily respond slower to many RT Actions because the antidepressants can make it more difficult to access Resource States. These clients may still benefit greatly from RT Actions, although the speed of their improvement may be affected.

Antidepressants may completely block some Resource States. For example, occasionally a client suffering from OCD will discover an antidepressant can eliminate OCD symptoms. When this occurs, the antidepressant is blocking from the Conscious the Vaded State that is the root of OCD avoiding behavior. The Retro Avoiding State has no need to carry out OCD avoiding behavior when this Vaded State is being blocked chemically. Of course, it is better to resolve the issues of the Vaded State, when possible, without the use of chemical intervention.

I will sometimes tell clients that when they, and their doctors, decide that it is time to cut back or stop the use of antidepressants that I would like to see them if they begin experiencing emotional setbacks. As states that were chemically blocked begin to surface RT actions may be used to resolve their issues.

Antidepressants do not block all states. RT Actions may be used with any client using antidepressants. Therapeutic intervention for some clients goes more slowly, while for other clients therapeutic intervention seems to not be affected by the use of antidepressants.

Below are the steps for working with a client with depression. The key is to resolve the state Vaded with Disappointment.

140

6.1.7   Vaded with Disappointment

States Vaded with Disappointment block other states. They operate like a semitrailer turned crossways on the freeway. They do not let other states enjoy anything. States may be Vaded with Disappointment about one particular issue, or about life in general. A person in a partnered relationship may discover that their partner has had an affair. The offended partner may have a state so disappointed that it will block all other states from enjoying the relationship. In this example, only states involved in the relationship may be blocked, as the person may be able to operate almost normally at work and with friends.

Psychological depression occurs when a Resource State becomes so disappointed that it blocks all states from enjoying living. In order to assist a client to change the blocking behavior of the state Vaded with Disappointment it is important to express to that state in a way that it can feel understood. If it does not feel understood by you then it may not cooperate in therapy.

Another aspect of working with a client who is depressed is the speed that work can progress. While psychological depression is caused psychosomatically, there is also a physiological component. The body physiologically slows down and it appears to take at least several days for energy to be restored to the body. As energy is restored to the body, work can progress more easily.

A step to help a client who has psychological depression is to find two resources that have enjoyed activities in the past, and that are willing to enjoy them again, then to gain permission from the depressed Resource State for them to begin that enjoyment.

The depressed Resource State will allow this to happen, and will cooperate, if it feels understood and appreciated by the therapist.

Steps for working with a state Vaded with Disappointment

1. There must be a determination that the Vaded State suffers from disappointment, as characterized by an exhibition of malaise; the shutting down of energy, and an inability to engage in life activities with enjoyment or excitement. (Action 1 – Diagnosis)

2. Two Resources should be located that have previously experienced enjoyment or excitement in an activity which would still be possible for the client to engage in.

3. A time when one of these activities was enjoyed should be revivified until it is obvious that the client is experiencing a level of joy or excitement within the imagery. (Action 8 – Find Resource, see page 56)

4. A name for that Resource should be negotiated and that Resource should be asked if it would be willing to again engage positively in the activity that it had in the past, if internal permission can be gained.

5. Step three and four should also be completed for the second Resource in step two.

6. The Resource that is Vaded with Disappointment should be brought to the Conscious and permission should be gained from that state for the two Resources to reengage in the activities they have enjoyed in the past.

7. Work should proceed with the Resource Vaded with Disappointment to determine its purpose and find adjusted or new roles where it can continue to fulfil that purpose. (Retro State Negotiation, Action 10, see page, 130)

Work should proceed with the Resource Vaded with Disappointment to determine its purpose and find adjusted or new roles where it can continue to fulfil that purpose.

Using RT Action 8, Find Resource

An important step in helping a depressed client regain energy is to find a Resource that has enjoyed an activity in the past. This is not as easy to do as it sounds. Depressed clients will often say they had never enjoyed anything in the past. But, if you ask the client to search his or her memory and intellectually remember something that was enjoyed, the client will be able to do this. A difference in using the Find Resource Action with non-depressed clients and using this Action with the depressed client is the difficulty the client has in remembering something that was enjoyed in the past.

When the client is able to remember a specific time that was enjoyed in the past, that time can be vivified until the energy of the client changes. When the client shows the positive energy of enjoying the activity, a name can be obtained for that Resource State, and it can be asked if it would be willing to enjoy that activity again if it gets permission to do that from the state that is upset.

Using RT Action 8, Find Resource

The same process described above needs to be completed with a second Resource State that has been able to enjoy something in the past, and that is willing to again enjoy that activity when granted permission.

At the end of the second Find Resource Action you will have two resources that have agreed to reengage with activities that they have enjoyed in the past (if they are granted permission to do that).

Using RT Action 10, Retro State Negotiation

The next step is to engage with the depressed Resource State. It is easy to find the state, because it dominates the personality. All you will need to do is ask the client to describe a recent emotional experience. It will be the depressed Resource State that describes this experience.

It is good to thank this state for speaking with you, show understanding for its level of despair, let it know it has a right to feel upset, and then ask it, even though it is upset if it would be willing for the two states that you just spoke with to reengage and enjoy what they do. You can tell the disappointed state that you want to work with it, not so things will be like they were in the past, but so it can make a positive contribution in the future.

This is about all that can be done in the first session of working with someone who has a Resource State suffering from Disappointment. The depressed person exhibits an obvious low level of energy. There is nothing that can be done in a single session that will dramatically change this. It takes time for this energy level to increase.

When the client returns the next week there is normally a marked improvement in energy, although it is often still low. The increased level of energy improves the chances of having a positive outcome when working with the Resource State that is Vaded with Disappointment.

Depending on what caused the state to feel disappointment, Retro State Negotiation can be used in a way that will either reduce responsibility of the Vaded State or find a new responsibility for that state. During this work it is important that the therapist continue to show respect that things will not be as they were, while at the same time indicating that the state that had been Vaded with Disappointment is important and it is important that it continue to contribute.

When the state that has been Vaded with Disappointment finds a way to accomplish its purpose through alternative activities, the client will show marked improvement. Focus should be on the purpose of the state, "What is your role? What is the purpose of what you have done in the past? How have you helped this person in the past?"

When you find the purpose of the state then you can find a new alternative way that state can accomplish that purpose. Again, it is most important not to indicate that things will be as good as they were. It is important to indicate that the state can contribute in a meaningful way.

Often clients will be misdiagnosed with depression. It is not unusual for a client to come to therapy that is suffering from a State Vaded with Fear, Rejection, or Confusion, who has been diagnosed with depression. If it becomes clear that a Resource State has been Vaded with Fear, Rejection, or Confusion, follow the treatment regimens associated with those pathologies.

6.1.8   Keeping purpose and trading purviews

This is an important concept for working with Retro States or states Vaded with Disappointment. These States are powerful and they believe what they do is highly important. The best way to help them change to preferred behavior is to complement them on the hard work they do to achieve their important purpose. The Resource State name they receive should relate to their purpose. They should be able to keep that name and that purpose and find a new way to achieve that purpose (a new purview) if they are needed in the future.

Therefore, it is highly important to find their purpose, "How do you help this person? What would happen if you did not help this person? What is your purpose?"

Praise the purpose and find a new way that purpose can be achieved with a positive behavior. Show an appreciation for the value of the purpose and plead with the state to continue to fulfill its purpose. Get at least one other state to show appreciation for the new behavior, and compliment the state that is taking on this behavior. This helps the state feel like taking on new behavior.

6.2 Skills for Day 6

Practice: Retro State Negotiation - Note: For Retro Avoiding States you must do the Vaded State work first

6.2.1 Retro State Negotiation

1. Vivify Specific to bring the state that performs the unwanted behavior to the conscious.
2. Show respect and appreciation.
3. Find its purpose, name it accordingly, and devise a preferred behavior that would fulfil the purpose.
4. Ask the state that did not like the behavior to say directly to the Retro State **how it will like it** with the new behavior.
5. and, if appropriate, find another state (Find Resource) to help with times the old behavior was evident.
6. Do an Imagery Check.

For video examples go to www.tinyurl.com/learnresourcetherapy.

6.3 Quiz and Activities for Day 6 Training

6.3.1 Quiz

1. What is the difference between a Retro Original and a Retro Avoiding State?

2. Is a state Vaded with Confusion or Vaded with Disappointment most closely associated with depression?

3. Why do some people have addictions?

4. What is the difference between a physical addiction and a psychological addiction?

5. Is OCD more associated with depression or addiction?

6. What type of pathological state is associated with addiction?

7. Why is Retro State Negotiation used to help someone who is depressed?

8. Why is Find Resource used to help someone who is depressed?

9. How should a state Vaded with disappointment be spoken with by the therapist?

10. What type of pathological state is associated with rage behavior?

6.3.2   Activity

Describe when it is important to work with a Vaded State in order to stop Retro Behavior, and when this is not important.

_____

_____

_____

_____

Why is it important to do Retro State Negotiation after resolving the associated Vaded State when working with a client who has Retro Avoiding behavior?

_____

_____

_____

_____

7 Day 7 RT Mapping & Ethics

One of the most popular techniques in Resource Therapy is Resource State Mapping, both for the clients and for the therapists. Mapping serves several purposes, it can be used as a check-up to see how the different Resources are doing, and it can be used to be informative for the client, to understand which Resources are available for any given time or activity. It is also a central part of Couples Therapy, with each partner using a Resource Mapping to learn about themselves and their partner so they can relate with the best parts for the benefit of the relationship.

Couples counselling works to improve communication, knowledge of strengths, and an understanding about states that can enjoy the relationship. During this therapy it is important to locate pathological states that have made communication and enjoyment difficult or impossible. Mapping is the tool that makes this possible.

Ethical Guidelines are also reviewed and discussed in Day 7. A short definition of the day seven terms is provided below. Make sure you are comfortable with the fuller meaning of these terms by the end of this day's training.

7.1 Core Concepts for Day 7 Training

Page		Page
Ethics: Confidentiality	What is Confidentiality, its importance, and when it should be breached?	148
Ethic: Duel Relationships	What are Duel Relationships and what are the considerations relating to them?	149

7.1 Core Concepts for Day 7 Training		
Active Listening	Hearing the whole message of what was said and reflecting it back to the client.	150
Resource Mapping	Sessions for the purpose to provide the client with information about his or her Resources, and to check their condition.	150
RT Couples Counselling	Therapy to insure that Resources States are healthy enough for a good relationship, to improve communication, and to provide mapping information to both partners.	159

7.1.1 Ethics: Confidentiality

Therapists should not discuss client cases with anyone other than supervisors, supervisees, or other professionals working in the same capacity at the same workplace, full stop. Confidential cases may be presented for training, and articles, or in books as long as there can be no identification of the person who is the client. Confidentiality should not otherwise be breached unless there is a need to breach it to protect the client or someone else who the client may be putting in danger. There is always a fuzzy area in terms of when to breach confidentiality, i.e., it is obvious that confidentiality should be breached if someone's life is in danger, and it is obvious it should not be breached if the danger is that a person could catch the common cold. Somewhere between catching a common cold and someone's life being in danger, the decision has to be made exactly where it should be breached. Therefore, it is necessary for the therapist to be an ethical person, and make this decision with the welfare of the client and others in mind.

7.1.2   Ethics: Duel Relationships

It is best for a therapist to take on a client when the client and the therapist have no other relationship between them. Other considerations need to be included in this discussion. It is often the case that training therapists will train with family members or friends, and this is considered okay. If it is clear that a person who is known will not be able to gain any other therapeutic relief, an ethical decision must be made as to the benefit to the client in offering therapy, even if a dual relationship exists.

Obviously a therapist should never take advantage of any client, physically or in any other way: The therapeutic relationship should be highly honored. Clients come to therapists, often in a vulnerable condition, seeking help, and it is the responsibility of the therapist to look after the welfare of the client. Personal considerations of what the therapist would like, should not be central in making a decision about dual relationships. After therapy, should a therapist and the client ever decide to have a friendship, it should be made clear to the client that should any further therapy be needed, a different therapist should be obtained.

The only friendships that clients and therapists should ever have are where there is not an unbalanced relationship between them. In other words, it may be possible for two therapists to enter into a friendship following therapy, but not a therapist with a client who sees the therapist in a guru status or position of higher power. It is the responsibility of the therapist to make these decisions, as clients will often desire friendships with the therapist and these are often not advisable.

During Therapy, should a client show inappropriate interest in the therapist: a good technique is to tell the client that it is (for example - the third session), the session that aspects of therapy are reviewed. The therapist then can, nonchalantly, go over aspects of confidentiality and mention that the therapeutic boundary is very distinct and that there can never be any relationship other than therapist and client within that relationship. Broaching the topic in this way allows the client to get the message that a strong distinct therapeutic boundary exists, without embarrassing the client by bringing up the concern of the therapist that the client has unwarranted feelings.

Therapy Notes

It is important for therapists to keep notes that may be referred to: or that may be subpoenaed, and because they may be subpoenaed it is appropriate to refrain from putting information in the notes that clients may not want to be made public.

7.1.3   Active Listening

Active listening is reflecting back to the client what has been heard. This is often in the form of feelings. In other words, we do not necessarily reflect the content of the words clients say, but we reflect back to the clients the intuitive understanding that we have received from those words. During particular times in therapy this can help Resource States feel heard, understood, and can help those Resource States stay in the Conscious so that work may continue with them. Active listening is an important and good ability for therapists to have, and is therefore worth developing.

Actively listening to your client entails never asking questions and never giving suggestions, merely reflecting what has been heard, and reflecting states of confusion: For example, "I'm a little bit confused, you said that you and your partner have a good relationship, but I get a sense there's something upsetting about that relationship to you." Clients would rather clarify confusion than answer probing questions. While active listening is a good technique to learn, and while there are times when it is the best way to talk with the client, there will be many times that it is appropriate to ask a question and there may be times you even want to make a suggestion.

7.1.4   Resource Mapping

Resource Mapping is the process of learning which Resources a person has, the roles of the states, which states know other states, the nature of their communication, and available states to call into the Conscious so they can be used at the best times (Emmerson, 2003).

Some benefits of conducting a Resource Mapping

1.   To learn the range of Resources that are available to the person.

2. To assess the connections of the Resource States to ensure they are cooperating and are not in conflict.

3. To discover if there are states that are Vaded or Retro that need intervention.

4. To assist in self-understanding and self-esteem.

Normal Resource Therapy interventions for presented issues will involve some degree of Resource Mapping, as good notes should be kept with information concerning all Resources contacted, but these interventions differ from Resource Mapping sessions, as they entail only contacting a limited number of Resources and only to achieve the goals of therapy. There is not an effort to produce a more complete map of the client's Resource structure. Resource Mapping is to provide the client with information that may be useful in achieving higher performance, more satisfaction, greater enjoyment, and a healthier psyche.

During the process of mapping, trauma and/or poor communication between states may become evident. At these times, clients who have asked specifically for mapping sessions should be asked if they wish to extend the scope of the sessions to therapeutic intervention. Most normally, clients want to attend to issues as they arise, therefore it is difficult to know the number of sessions a mapping may take.

It appears to be impossible to do a self-mapping. We need the assistance of another therapist to discover our states, at least our Underlying States.

The client needs to decide how detailed a Resource mapping is preferred, and this decision can be amended at any time. This decision will entail a balancing between time and money, and the level of self-awareness and work on issues desired. The fee for mapping sessions is normally somewhat higher than a normal consultation fee, as a written map presentation needs to be prepared for the client.

Process

Discussion with each state is limited, mainly to 1) role, 2) name, 3) knowledge of other states, 4) attitude toward other states, and 5) willingness to help either in communication or role.

1. Select any Resource State

2. Vivify Specific when that Resource has come out, and then snowball from it to other States. This means ask it what other Resources it knows, and write down those States.

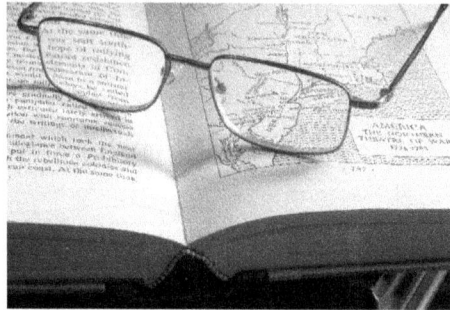

3. When the Resource is speaking, gather info on 1) Role, 2) Name, 3) Knowledge of other states, 4) Attitudes toward other states, 5) willingness to help.

4. Then, move to one of the other states it knows and continue the mapping, gathering this info about each State.

5. Always move to a state from a state that has knowledge of it. This means that when moving to states you may need to return to a state you have already spoken with in order to get to a state that other states do not know.

(Select the first State) The first step in Resource Mapping is to gain access to any Resource States by using the Vivify Specific Action. It is helpful to have large, blank sheets of paper available. The name of each state can be circled during a mapping session. A line should be drawn from each state to the other states it knows.

7.1.5 Role

(Role) When talking with a Resource State first ask about its function or role. This provides useful information for Resource naming.

7.1.6 Name

(Name) Next ask the Resource what you can call it. It is a good idea to circle the name it prefers. This makes it easy to quickly locate the name on a page that will become full of words, lines, and arrows.

It is not unusual for a state to have some difficulty choosing a name, and it may be necessary to suggest a name yourself, but always check that the name you choose is acceptable with the state with which you are speaking. For example, if the role of the state is to tidy and clean, you might ask the state if you could call it "Cleaner." It is important to get a name for each of the states you speak with so that you can easily call the state out again whenever needed. This also provides a reference to the state for communication with other states.

You will be able to ask other states if they know "Cleaner." Always give the state the first opportunity to name itself, and do not assign a name to a state without first checking that the state is happy to accept the name. Occasionally, a state will give itself a negative name, such as "Dummy." When this happens I attempt to see if there is a less negative name that the state will be happy with, but if the state is reluctant to change the name, I will accept the negative name. In therapy it is often the case that a state that first gave itself a negative sounding name, later wants to change the name to something more positive, to reflect a change in how it feels.

I do not accept negative behavior names for a state. For example, I would not accept the name 'Smoker'. I would ask the state what its purpose is, how it helps the client. A state that currently smokes might help by being a 'Rebel', by being a 'Socializer', by helping 'Relax', or by helping the client to 'Escape'. Remember, do not let a different state name a Resource. The first state you speak with may say it knows a lazy state, but when that state is given an opportunity to name itself it may name itself, 'Recharger'.

7.1.7   Knowledge and impressions of other states

(Knowledge of other states) Most Resources communicate frequently with one or more other states. It is useful in mapping Resources to discover which states each Resource knows and communicates with. "What other states do you know?" can be a revealing question.

Another technique is to ask the Conscious state if it knows states you have already discovered. I like to draw a pencil line between the circled names and the states that they communicate with. There will often be clusters of states that know each other well, and work together, and they may be quite separate from other states or clusters of states. There are often surface and Underlying States that have no knowledge of the existence of some underlying Resources. Sometimes even Surface States do not know each other, as is the case when a person cannot remember the last few minutes of driving, or some other activity, like reading a paragraph.

(Attitude toward other states) Along the pencil line that connects states that know or communicate together I write comments about how the states think and feel about each other. Above the line I put an arrow in one direction and below the line I put an arrow in the other direction. This allows me to know the feeling of each state toward the other. For example, if the state 'Protector' dislikes 'Hedonist,' above the line I would make a note of this with the arrow pointing from 'Protector' to 'Hedonist.' Below the line the arrow would point in the opposite direction with comments on the attitude 'Hedonist' holds toward 'Protector.'

7.1.8   What it can offer in the future

(Willingness to help) An important part of mapping is discovering how the different states would like to be helpful. It is useful information for the client to learn about a state that has skills in assertiveness. A wise state may be asked to call upon either the state that can be assertive or a state that can show more anger, depending on the situational need. Resource Mapping can inform clients of their potential and give them the information to reach toward that potential.

What to give to the Client

Following a Resource Mapping the notes should be typed so the client can have a copy of the information gained during the mapping. I use a table format, where the name of the Resource is followed by its role, the other states it knows, its attitude about those states, and how it may be able to be useful to the client. There is a table for each Resource State that has been mapped.

Clients love the process of Resource Mapping and the information they receive from it. When Resource Mapping is used in couple's therapy, both individuals seem to enjoy seeing and talking about both their map and the map of their partner.

154

Following a mapping session a table, such as the one below, can be used for each state in order to provide the client with information about the states that were mapped. Obviously, the number of rows will depend on the number of other states each state reports knowing.

State Name	Purpose or role
Other States it knows	What it thinks about each State
How it can help	

Advantages of a Resource Mapping

There are several advantages people gain from learning about their Resources. A number of my clients have said they feel much better in just knowing who they are and why they are the way they are. When we experience our own states and feel what each state feels it is a self-revelation. Some clients have said they thought they were crazy, the way their mood changed in a seemingly random fashion. When they learned their states, and the role of each state, it made sense to them. They felt empowered and better able to be in control in their lives. The following section will deal with how learning your Resources can increase personal development, and our ability to enjoy life.

Personal Development with Resource Therapy

Knowing and having access to our states can benefit our personal development in several ways. Some of the assets include:

1. We can safely experience the emotional depths of childhood, regardless of our age.

2. We can feel love.

3. We can become assertive at appropriate times.

4. We can be angry at appropriate times.

5. We can be confident in speaking.

6. We can face criticism without feeling abused.

7. We can be our logical self when it is appropriate.

8. We can be our party self when it is appropriate.

9. We can experience better physical health.

A safe hug while in a fragile, child state, is an extraordinary experience. It is felt and appreciated deeply. A hug while in an intellectual state feels cold and uneasy. Imagine what it would be like having to live in a single Resource. Consider Paul, who is stuck in a head/rational state. Paul responds to everything rationally. There is no evident confusion over choice, since there is only the rational choice. There are no evident feelings of joy, fear, love, or hate. There is no excitement or feelings of awe and wonder. There is just "getting down to business," just evenness, just a low level of emotion. There are some Pauls out there, who have learned to stay in one or two states almost all the time, to the detriment of their ability to enjoy living.

What defines us is our feelings, our ability to experience love, awe, wonder, fear, and even hate. We are emotional people in a wonderfully emotional world. Too often, we lose the ability to be a child, or to think of what we want, rather than what we "should" have. We are made up of a large number of Resources with a wide variety of potentials. Our most enjoyable states are the child states. It takes a combination of courage and wisdom to be able to readily access them. While they are our most enjoyable states, they are also states that should only be called out when it is safe, otherwise they can feel over-exposed and may refuse to come out at all. Therefore, we need our assertive states too.

As we age, many of us learn that it is easier to stay away from some of the more fragile child states that have the capacity to really get excited, to love, and to be amazed, but also have the capacity to feel hurt, and fear. We not only have these fragile inner states, but we have states whose role it is to protect them; states that are a bit hard and crusty, with a shell. Learning our states allows us the ability to allow a fragile child state into the Conscious to experience the 'wow' of a hug, love, awe, taste, and more, when it is safe. A wise state can be called upon to act as the traffic director to see if the time is safe to allow the child state into the Conscious, and to decide when the child state should be protected by calling out a tougher, protector state. The goal is to experience powerful feelings, without feeling exposed, or overexposed.

We can learn that it is safe to call out a fragile child state (all child states are not fragile) when we are with someone who we can trust. It is important to learn to expose fragile states only when it is safe, and allow the protector states to do their job when it is not safe. It would not be good to expose a fragile state to someone who would likely hurt it. This would make it more difficult for that state to become Conscious the next time. The more a state is hurt, the less it is willing to come out. This is why it is useful to use a wise state to determine the safety of allowing a fragile child state to come out.

I, personally, have a state that is so fragile I have learned to call it out only when I am with someone I have great trust with, and then only when my eyes are closed. When I have great trust and get a loving hug I can call this state out, and the experience is incredible. It feels like a very young state (started when I was young), so I have named it "Infant." If I stay in "Infant" and open my eyes I can feel over-exposed. My wise state understands this and only calls infant out when it is safe to feel that wonderful flow of love from someone I trust. If I am with people whose purpose is something I question, my wise state calls out a nice hard, crusty, assertive state that can handle hardship; a state with a nice thick crust that can keep the barbs from penetrating to my fragile parts.

How many States to know?

Resource mapping will probably never result in all Resources being mapped or known. It is up to the individual how extensive a mapping is desired. Most of the Surface States, the states that often become Conscious, and some Underlying States may be mapped in a single session. A single session of Resource Mapping will generally result in the client and the therapist becoming familiar with 5 to 15 states. Becoming familiar with this number of states, especially with common Surface States, can be enriching for the client. We have a much larger number of states.

Some clients will wish to gain a fuller understanding of their Resource structure, and learn about their Underlying States. These Underlying States affect us occasionally, and often possess assets that we seldom gain benefit from. These Underlying States may be accessed by Vivifying Specific times when the client has felt young or fragile. Learning about these states will give the client a fuller understanding of their personality, their strengths, and their resources. It will also provide the client with a rather detailed history of experiences, since allowing Underlying States expression brings to the surface experiences of those childhood states. It is important to note that the memories of any Resource may not be totally accurate. This is true for both Surface States and Underlying States.

A more complete Resource Mapping will take several sessions, especially if issue processing is undertaken. It will result in the client gaining a keen understanding of self. It will allow the person to be more fully functioning, even when issue processing is not undertaken. This more complete mapping results in the same kind of awareness that psychoanalysts hope to achieve during the course of analysis. Resource Mapping allows this result in a few sessions, while psychoanalysis requires many sessions over a few years.

It is not unusual for trauma to be uncovered during Resource Mapping, regardless of the detail of the mapping. When this occurs it is incumbent upon the therapist to ask the client if he or she would like to process that trauma. When a client has come for mapping, and has not indicated a desire to work on issues, a verbal contract is needed before issue processing is undertaken. Often the mapping may proceed and the client can decide after the session about returning to work on the issues that may have become evident. Occasionally, a prime opportunity exists during

the session to process issues. The client may be asked immediately if this is something that would be preferred. It should be noted that bringing forth a trauma and not processing it will leave the client feeling closer to the experience of the trauma. It is preferred to process trauma, rather than to leave it unprocessed, although this should always be the decision of the client.

7.1.9   RT Couples Counselling

RT Couples Counselling is to help partners communicate better, to help each person to attain a level of mental health necessary for a good relationship, and to help partners gain renewed access to the states that previously enjoyed the relationship.

The four stages of RT Couples Counselling

1. **First Session Together:** The couple will define issues and times of poor communication. During the first session the couple will come in together and tell about each aspect of their difficulty. The therapist should take good notes on this to ensure that parts that are having difficulty communicating can be mapped during the mapping sessions.

2. **Single sessions:** Each partner will come for mapping, ensuring parts are mapped that are involved in the disputes, parts are mapped that can communicate better, and parts are mapped that have enjoyed the relationship. Pathological states need to be attended to during these sessions. These mapping sessions may last from one session to several. These are individual sessions, without both parties being present. It is common, during these mapping sessions, for the Vaded, Retro, Conflicted and Dissonant states to become evident. These states need to be brought back to normality for the benefit of the relationship; therefore, the single sessions may last a few weeks.

3. **Negotiation:** When the couple comes back in together each person is given their map and a copy of their partner's map. Couples seem to enjoy seeing their Resource States and their partner's Resource States. A negotiation needs

to occur to assist couples in having preferred states out, especially during times when difficult things are discussed. It is good for each partner to have in their Resource map an intellectual state that has the ability to hear criticism and intellectually assess it, without being reactive.

4. **Trial:** The final phase is for the couple to go home to practice having the right states out. A good technique is for each partner to allow the other to finish saying everything that they want to say, before it is the other person's turn to talk. When the couple returns to therapy, if the communication is still problematic, the therapist should have the couples attempt to communicate during the session so the therapist will be able to suggest a better Resource State to hear and respond. The Find Resource Action may be necessary to find a needed Resource. Before the end of this phase emphasis should be placed on bringing states out that enjoy the relationship.

7.2   Skills for Day 7

Practice Resource Mapping

7.2.1   Resource Mapping

1. Vivify Specific when a Resource has been out, and then snowball from it to other states. This means to ask it what other resources it knows, and write down those states.

2. When it is speaking, gather information on:

   1) Role

   2) Name

   3) Knowledge of other states

   4) Attitudes toward other states

   5) Willingness to help.

3. Then move to one of the other states it knows and continue the mapping, gathering this info about each state.

7.3 Quiz and Activities for Day 7 Training

7.3.1 Quiz

1. When should client confidentiality be breached?

2. What are two benefits of Resource Mapping?

3. How is Resource Mapping used in the relationship counselling?

4. How often are questions asked during active listening?

5. How often are suggestions given during active listening?

6. What is the value of active listening?

7. Why is it appropriate to charge more for a Resource Mapping session?

8. What should the therapist do, when during a Resource Mapping session a state appears with a psychological issue?

9. What do we mean by dual relationships when talking about ethics in Therapy?

10. Is it likely that all states will be mapped during a Resource Mapping session?

7.3.2 Activity

Fill out the following two tables for two of your own Resource States.

State Name	Purpose or role	
	Other States it knows	What it thinks about the State
	How it can help	

State Name	Purpose or role	
	Other States it knows	What it thinks about the State
	How it can help	

8 Day 8 Pain & Somatic Presentations

The eighth day of training covers both how to deal with resistant parts, and how to help clients with pain and somatic symptoms. Resistance in therapy is merely a part that is protecting a more fragile part, or a part that is afraid of letting a fragile part into the Conscious. RT techniques help resistant parts ally with the therapist in order to prevent it from fighting the therapy process.

Pain and Somatic symptoms can be cause by Resource States (psychosomaticly) or they can be purely physical in origin. Day 8 training gives therapists tools to help determine both the nature of the symptoms and to reduce or eliminate them whether they are psychosomatic or organic.

A short definition of the day eight terms is provided below. You should make sure you are comfortable with the fuller meaning of these terms by the end of this day's training.

8.1 Core Concepts for Day 8 Training

Page		Page
Pain and Somatic Symptoms	These are physical pains or any physiological complaint.	164
Organic Symptoms	Symptoms that are caused purely by physiology, such as the pain from a bee sting.	165
Psychosomatic Symptoms	Symptoms that are caused by a Resource State, such as a tension headache.	165

8.1 Core Concepts for Day 8 Training		
How to tell?	It is useful to distinguish if a symptom is caused organically or psychosomatically to choose the most appropriate intervention.	165
Organic Intervention	This intervention uses the abilities of a Resource State to take on some, or all, of the sensations so a surface state does not have to have such a negative experience.	167
Psychosomatic Intervention	This intervention locates the state causing the symptom and ensures it no longer has to create it.	168
Action 13 Resistance Alliancing	Handling resistance by allying with the resistant part.	169
Acknowledgement, Appreciation and Suggestion	Handling resistance by showing respect to the protecting resistant part.	169
Engagement Method	Engaging directly with the resistant part to be able to continue.	170

8.1.1 Pain and Somatic Symptoms

In 1990, with the article, *Dissociation and displacement: where goes the "ouch?"*, John and Helen Watkins demonstrated that when the hypnotized client receives a suggestion that a pain will not be felt, even though the surface state may report experiencing no pain, an underlying state does feel that pain. This underlying state can cause the client later psychological or physical issues. It can become Vaded. It is therefore important to understand appropriate techniques for dealing with pain and somatic symptoms when using therapeutic interventions.

If the client has not had a medical examination in relation to a physiological pain or symptom, it is appropriate to have the client to seek a medical opinion prior to a Resource Therapy intervention.

Pain and Somatic symptoms may be organic or psychosomatically based. Therapeutic techniques are required to both assess 1) if a symptom is organic or psychosomatically based, and 2) how to safely intervene to moderate or eliminate the symptoms of each. Organic symptoms require the recruitment of a strong underlying state, while psychosomatic symptoms require Vaded State resolution.

8.1.2   Organic Symptoms

A pain or a somatic symptom from an Organic Cause is not caused by a Resource State. It is purely physiological. A tooth being drilled is an example of an Organic Root cause. It is obvious that the pain is coming from the drill touching a nerve in the tooth. A bee sting is another good example.

8.1.3   Psychosomatic Symptoms

A pain or a somatic symptom from a Psychosomatic Cause is being created by a Resource State for a reason. It may still be able to be physically measured, but it is being caused by a state.

A pain or somatic symptom may have an Organic Root, but may be moderated or exacerbated by a Resource State. Some symptoms may not appear without the intervention of a Resource State, even when there is a physical cause. Some epileptic seizures are examples of this. A person who is organically prone to seizures may only have them when psychologically stressed.

8.1.4   How to tell?

When determining the appropriate psychological intervention an important aspect to consider is whether symptoms are based in a psychological root cause, or a physiological root cause. Tension headache is a good example of a symptom that is based in a psychological root cause. The psychological tension results in constriction of muscles that in turn results in a headache.

It is important to clarify that psychosomatically based pain or somatic symptoms often become organic, and measurable. For example, merely being stressed brings about the release of epinephrine. This is the same hormone commonly called adrenaline, and its release brings about a number of physiologically measurable changes. Digestion slows, the production of antibodies slows, and blood flow to the extremities of the hands and feet slows causing finger temperature to decrease. These are just a few of the physiologically measurable reactions to psychological stress.

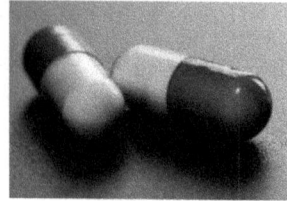

Ways to determine if pain or illness is Organic or Psychologically-based

If the pain or illness is situationally based, in other words if it happens during certain times, but not during other times (e.g., "It happens when I go to town but it doesn't happen when I am at home"), then it is most likely to be a pain or illness that is psychosomatically based.

If the pain or illness happens randomly then it may be either organically based or psychosomatically based. Disturbances that are almost always organically based include schizophrenia, manic depression, ADHD, and injuries.

Disturbances that are often, at least partially, psychosomatically-based include, both tension headaches and migraine headaches, irritable bowel syndrome, endometriosis, asthma, and any situationally based symptom.

If it is unclear if a symptom is based on an Organic Root or a Psychosomatic Root the first intervention should assume a Psychosomatic Root. The reason for this is simple. If a Resource State is causing a symptom for a reason, and if another Resource State attempts to take on the sensations of that symptom in order to spare Surface States from the discomfort, the causal Resource State will be frustrated and just try harder to create the symptom. Two states would be working against each other.

8.1.5   Organic Intervention

If the pain or somatic symptom is organically based, it is important to ensure that enough of the pain is continued to be experienced to keep the client safe. We do not want to eliminate a pain that is an indicator for further medical attention.

When it is clear that an organically caused pain is not benefiting the client, a good technique to reduce the sensation of that pain is to ask a brave underlying Resource State to take on the sensations so that the Conscious state does not have to. The underlying state that is willing to take on the pain may be trained to go through the Separation Sieve (Action 14) anytime it chooses to cleanse itself of any pain it has collected. This process may be used for the underlying state to take on only a portion of the pain so that the Conscious state can be aware of a smaller amount of sensation, in order to react appropriately. It is best to make sure the client returns to therapy, so that this brave underlying state can be returned to in order to determine that it is happy to continue with its important work of diverting pain sensations from reaching Conscious states.

Working with organically based Pain or Somatic Presentations

1. Have the client close their eyes and go into detail about the current vivified sensations of the pain or complaint. This should take a few minutes to ensure appropriate focus.
2. Ask for a name of the Resource State that is experiencing the unwanted symptoms or pain.
3. Thank that state for having taken on the symptoms so all other states would not have to.
4. Ask to speak with a brave and strong state that would be willing to volunteer to take on the sensations so the other states will not have to. This can be an underlying state or a surface state. If it is a surface state there will later be a dual awareness of the sensations, with the more Conscious state barely noticing them. If it is an underlying state, there may be little awareness of the sensations. The amount of awareness can be negotiated with the brave state, as there may be a need for some awareness.

5. Get a name for this state and praise the brave state and thank it for taking on such an important job. Let it know that other states will greatly appreciate its important role. Have at least one state speak directly to it, thanking it for helping.

6. Let it know that you will check on it to see how it is going. Teach it to go through the Separation Sieve (Action 14) anytime it chooses, and every night during sleep, in order to stay cleansed of any residue from the sensations.

7. Ask the client to return so you can check on the brave resource state to make sure it feels positive about its work, appreciated, and able to continue helping.

8.1.6 Psychosomatic Intervention

If a pain or somatic symptom is psychosomatically-based the best course of action is to ask the client to describe in great detail the exact sensations that are currently being experienced, and during that description, ask the client to describe what is currently being experienced emotionally. Bridging may then take place from the emotion to the ISE, and work may be done to resolve the Vaded State associated with the pain, or to resolve and negotiate with the Resource State that is creating the pain.

1. Have the client close eyes and go into detail about the current vivified sensations of the pain or complaint (Vivify Specific, Action 2).
2. Ask what emotion is being felt in the middle of this detailing.
3. Vivify the location in the body where that emotion is experienced.
4. Bridge (Action 3)
5. Resolve the associated Vaded State using Expression (Action 4), If Vaded with Rejection, Introject Speak (Action 5), Removal (Action 6), and Relief (Action 7).
6. If pain or illness was situationally based, use Find Resource (Action 8) to locate a Resource for that situation in the future, then Imagery Check (Action 12) to ensure the client is prepared to use this state.

8.1.7　Action 13: Resistance Alliancing

Resistance is caused by Protector Resources attempting to keep the therapist from bringing a Vaded State to the Conscious for resolution. These states do this in order to protect the client from the uncomfortable feelings of the Vaded State. Resistance Alliancing is used to form an alliance between the therapist and the protector state, so the protector state will allow the therapeutic process to continue.

There are two methods to assist protector states to allow the therapeutic process to continue, 1) Acknowledgement, Appreciation and Suggestion, and 2) Engagement. The first method works with most Protector States, but often an Intellectual Protector State, if there, will maintain its resistance. Therefore, if an Intellectual Protector State is evident it is best to use the Engagement intervention method.

8.1.8　Acknowledgement, Appreciation and Suggestion

This method consists of making a statement to the resistant Resource without starting a conversation with it. Protecting Resources see themselves as important. It is their job to keep the hurting state below the surface so the client will not have to experience feeling the feelings of the Vaded State. They work hard. Most of the time they will step aside, when their work is acknowledged as being important, and when it is suggested that now that the therapist is here, a much deserved rest can be taken.

When resistance is noticed a statement such as this can be made

"I can see there is a part there that is protecting a fragile part. I want to say thank you to that protecting part. I'm sure you have been protecting for a long time and that is very helpful. It must be very tiring to constantly be on guard. I am here to help too, and while I am here it might be a really good time for you to take a well-deserved rest. But, even though you are resting, keep an eye open just to make sure everything is alright."

This statement contains:

- **Acknowledgement** (I can see there is a part there that is protecting a fragile part.)
- **Appreciation** (I want to say thank you to that protecting part. I'm sure you have been protecting for a long time and that is very helpful. It must be very tiring to constantly be on guard.) and
- **Suggestion** (I am here to help too, and while I am here it might be a really good time for you to take a well-deserved rest. But, even though you are resting, keep an eye open just to make sure everything is alright.)

Imagine being an angry parent visiting your child's school. If you are told to calm down or leave, you may feel a need to get even angrier. Compare the difference with being told (Acknowledgement), "I can see you are upset," (Appreciation), "A lot of parents don't even come here, and the fact that you are here and upset tells me that you care a lot about your child. That makes me want to help," and (Suggestion), "Come in and sit down so you can tell me all about it."

The upset parent has a Resource that is out for a purpose. It will stay out as long as it feels it is needed. That angry Resource does not have to stay out when it feels acknowledged and appreciated. It is willing to listen to the suggestion that now is a safe time to take a rest and let another part talk. In the same way, the resistant part is out for a purpose, and when it can see that it is acknowledged and respected it most often allows therapy to continue without resistance.

Following Acknowledgement, Appreciation and Suggestion, work may immediately continue and most of the time the resistant part is happy to allow that to happen. If the resistant part is still evident then the next method of direct engagement may be employed.

8.1.9   Engagement Method

This method for allying with a resistant state may be used either for clients who seem to hide in intellectualizations, or for those who the first method proved unsuccessful. It is easy to understand. Like people, Resources are curious about what others think of them. If they say something or ask something, they are curious about how it was heard.

Therefore, the resistant state can be engaged with directly. For example, if a client continues to intellectualize during the Vivify Specific Action when you are attempting to bring out an emotional Vaded State you can say:

"This part I am speaking with right now seems like a good thinking part. Can I call this part of you, 'Head'? (yes) 'Head', thank you for talking with me. I know you are aware of that fragile part that we have been talking about. What do you think of it? Do you like it, or do you just wish it would go away?"

Regardless of how the question is answered, the next step is to say:

"Alright, I just wonder what that state feels about what you just said. Fragile part, 'Head' just said *'whatever Head had said'*. How does that make you feel? I bet that makes you feel (either good or bad, depending on what the other state said), doesn't it?"

At this point two things happen. 1) 'Head' wants to know what the fragile part feels about what it said, so 'Head' sits back and listens, without blocking, and 2) the Fragile part is given a direct opportunity to answer an easy question.

When the Fragile part answers the question, immediately thank it for talking with you, get a name for it, and continue to call it by that name, thus holding it in the Conscious.

8.2 Skills for Day 8

8.2.1 Practice: Pain or Somatic Symptoms

1. Have the client close eyes and go into detail about the current or vivified sensations of the pain or somatic complaint.

2. Ask what emotion is being felt in the middle of this detailing.

3. Vivify the location in the body where that emotion is experienced.

4. Bridge

5. Resolve the associated Vaded State using Expression, Removal, (Introject Speak), and Relief

6. If pain or illness was situationally based, use Find Resource to locate a Resource for that situation in the future, then Imagery Check.

8.3   Quiz and Activities for Day 8 Training

8.3.1   Quiz

1. Is a pain that is situationally based more likely to be organic or psychosomatic?

2. Is PTSD more likely to be organic or psychosomatic?

3. Is ADHD more likely to be organic or psychosomatic?

4. Is panic disorder more likely to be organic or psychosomatic?

5. Is psychosis more likely to be organic or psychosomatic?

6. Is manic-depression more likely to be organic or psychosomatic?

7. Is anorexia more likely to be organic or psychosomatic?

8. Why is it not advisable to suggest to a client that a pain will not be felt?

9. How can an underlying state be used to help a client control organic pain?

10. How do you help someone if the pain is considered to be psychosomatic?

8.3.2   Activity Question

There is an important sequence for the selectin of treatment for pain or somatic symptoms. After it is clear that the symptom does not need medical intervention, which of the following is better, and why?

- If you are not sure if the cause is organic or psychosomatic start with the organic treatment intervention.

- If you are not sure if the cause is organic or psychosomatic, start with the psychosomatic intervention.

See the last paragraph in How to tell?, page 165

9 Day 9 The Separation Sieve & What Lies Within?

The Separation Sieve is one of the most useful techniques. It is a metaphoric tool that allows a safe trial for letting something go, before deciding to do so. It can be used as a replacement for Bridging and for the Actions 3 thru 7, if the therapist is having difficulty bridging. It is useful for helping clients decide what they want to release and to hang onto following a relationship

A further useful technique in Day 9 is learning how to work with OPIs. The Separation Sieve is part of that work. OPIs are unusual manifestations that actually claim to not be a part of the client. Interestingly they can be negotiated with to leave, and afterward clients gain psychological benefit.

There is a review in Day 9 of the various parts that can be encountered while working with a parts therapy. A short definition of the day nine terms is provided below. You should make sure you are comfortable with the fuller meaning of these terms by the end of this day's training.

9.1 Core Concepts for Day 9 Training

Page #'s are Hyperlinks on eBooks.		Page
What lies within?	Five manifestations within the personality.	176
Resource State	A physiological part of the personality. Part of self.	177
Introject	An internalized impression held by a Resource State.	178

9.1 Core Concepts for Day 9 Training		
Inner Self	A part that everyone has, sometimes quite underlying.	181
Creative Form Identity (CFI)	A Resource State represented in a creative manner.	182
Other Personalized Introject (OPI)	An uncommon Introject claiming personhood. It can leave with appropriate negotiation.	185
Action 14 The Separation Sieve	A metaphoric technique allowing a focused intent to let go of something.	188
OPI Intervention	A technique that assists an OPI to leave the psyche.	191

9.1.1   What lies within?

The psyche is fascinating, and in this section 5 different personality manifestations are discussed. They are evidenced, some often and some rarely, while working with Resource States. To be a complete therapist it is most appropriate to be aware of what might manifest and to have a theoretical understanding and therapeutic interventions that help the client to become empowered and mentally healthy.

The following 5 variations may manifest when working with parts. It is most appropriate to become familiar with each, both in relation to theory and to intervention.

What lies within

- Resource States
- Introjects
- Inner Self
- Creative Form Identities (CFIs)
- Other Personalized Introjects (OPIs)

9.1.2   Resource State

In psychology, there has long been a debate about what is nature and what is nurture, what is heredity and what is environment. Our Resource States come from training, from our living, from our nurture. While how we are born, our nature, impacts upon the types of Resource States we develop, all Resource States are developed as a result of our life situations.

We may be born naturally to be more bold, or less bold, more conservative or less conservative, and that will impact on the types of Resource States we develop.

When we do something over and over again as a coping mechanism to a life situation we grow a neural bundle of fibers, a neural pathway and that is a Resource State. We use these Resource States in a way that best suits us. So, our Resource States are parts of our brain, physiological, and have been created by the way that we have coped with life situations. Resource States have their own special traits.

Resource State traits

- They are created by repetition usually in childhood.
- They are a physiological part of the brain.
- They cannot be destroyed and they cannot leave.
- They can slightly change their role, and they can change the amount they come out.
- They are our inner resources.
- They are what we Bridge to and go to when they are vaded.
- We can feel an inner peace when they respect each other and get along.

- They can be Vaded, when they carry unresolved issues from the past.

- They can be Retro, when they continue with a role that is not wanted.

- They can be Conflicted, when they do not respect other Resource States.

- They can be Dissonant, when they are Conscious at the wrong time.

- They can be Normal, when they are relaxed and they help us externally and get along internally.

9.1.3 Introject

Introjects are fairly easy to understand. They are our internalized impressions of other people. We have Introjects of everyone we know, and even everyone we imagine. If we know someone or can imagine a person we can play act that person just like an actor in a movie can pretend to be someone else.

An interesting thing about Introjects is that each one of our Resource States has its very own Introjects of other people. This is why you may find yourself liking someone in one Resource State and not liking that same person while you are in another Resource State. For example, you may have a Resource State that is fragile and needs love. This Resource State may really want a relationship with someone who gives it love. But another Resource State that is more intellectual may not have respect for that other person because they are not challenging.

While you are in one Resource State you may feel, "I love you," and while in the other Resource State you may feel like you really have to get out of this relationship. Each of the two Resource States have their own different Introject for the same other person.

An abusive father may be loved by one Resource State and may be detested by the Resource State that has been abused by him. Here again the two Resource States have different Introjects for the same person, the father.

It is our Resource States that introject Introjects. In other words, each of our Resource States forms an internal impression of another person, and introjects the person into its memory.

We can have an Introject that we fear internally. This fear is really an illusionary fear because Introjects are not really real in a sense of something that can hurt us, other than the power that we give them inside. A real person can hit us and can hurt us, but an Introject of that person is just an internalized impression that we hold on the inside. It has no real power, other than the power we give it. The techniques in Day 5 to heal Vaded Resource States are to help Resource States that have held fear of Introjects to release their fear and feel supported, and to learn that there is nothing really there on the inside that can hurt. Sharing an internal unconditional love and an understanding hug from a nurturing Resource State, is a way they can learn the fearful Introject is past, over, obsolete and their internal space can be clear and free.

Our Resource States have Introjects of inspiring people, of people we love, of people we would like to be more like, and the people who we dislike and sometimes fear.

Probably none of our Introjects are entirely accurate. This makes sense because each of our Resource States holds different impressions of different people. It is obvious that they cannot all be accurate. It is probable that none of them are completely accurate. Therefore, our Introjects do not really represent another person completely and accurately. They still serve us well. We learn from them, we can love them, and we can be inspired by them.

We may learn from an Introject that the person who has been introjected should be avoided. That can be a good thing to learn. If someone is dangerous it is probably wise to avoid them.

But it is not wise to hold an internal fear that interferes with our day. The Resource State that holds an internal fear of an Introject is Vaded. We have learned that there is no reason for a Resource State to hold an internal fear, although it is useful for a Resource State to hold an understanding that a person may be dangerous, so that person can be avoided in life.

Any power that an Introject has within us was internally given to it by the Resource State that introjected it, that holds it internally. That is pretty exciting because Resource States have the ability to learn. We have seen how Resource States can learn that their inner space can be safe and supported. And the Resource State that had in the past feared an Introject can be given loving support by a nurturing state.

An intellectual Resource State may understand that Introjects are powerless, but a Vaded Resource State may still hold a fear of an Introject. That is why it is important for the Vaded state to be out when it learns empowerment and support.

While Introjects are internalized impressions of other people, we can also have Introjects of things that are not people. Obviously, we can have Introjects of our pets. We can even have Introjects of things like a storm. It is possible to hold a fear of a storm on the inside that has been introjected. We can also have an Introject of a beautiful stream.

Resource States may be vaded by Introjects of things that are not people. For example, a Resource State may hold an internalized fear of a wild animal, a storm, or anything else that has been introjected. It is not good to empower something on the inside that we do not want to empower, or that does not deserve to be empowered. It is appropriate to reclaim our internal power and for all of our Resource States to learn that the inside is a place of peace and safety, even if the outside may sometimes not be.

Understanding that the Introject has no power inside, allows the fearful Resource State to tell the Introject, "I do not want you in my inner space. Get out now." In this way the Resource State that was fearful, was Vaded, re-claims its power and is no longer Vaded.

Introject traits

- Introjects are created by a Resource State when it takes on an internalized impression.
- Each Resource State will have its own Introjects. One Resource State may like a person, and another Resource State may not like that same person. One Resource State may see a person as loving and another Resource State may see that same person as boring.
- Resource States may hold various emotions about Introjects. For example, a Resource State may love, respect, fear, or hate an Introject.
- A Vaded Resource State is vaded because of the impressions it holds about Introjects.
- A Resource State can learn that Introjects are merely internalized impressions and that they have no real power on the inside.

180

- Introjects may be asked to leave by a Resource State once the Resource State realizes the Introject is powerless.

- Because Introjects are merely internalized impressions they are not necessarily accurate representations. What is perceived about a person may or may not be accurate.

- Resource States may be empowered by positive Introjects, inspired by them, and can learn from them.

- It is possible for a Resource State to think about what an admired Introject would do to get inspiration in how to handle situations in life.

9.1.4 Inner Self

Inner Self is a part that has different traits than Resource States. It is the one part that everyone seems to have, and unlike Resource States it reports having always been there.

It is quite a distinct and interesting part. Inner self can appear to have access to information around the beginning of life or around the end of life. Some of you will have heard of near-death experiences (NDE). A lot has been written about these experiences by Elizabeth Kubler-Ross and others.

Some people, at a time when they appear clinically dead, having no heartbeat and no electrical brain activity, have reported that they were able to observe what was occurring to their body, often from the vantage point of floating above the body. Some of these people reported moving from their body to another room in the hospital or across the country, and they have been able to report accurate observations about what they had seen. Some people who have been blind since birth report accurately what they have seen visually during their NDE.

What is this conscious awareness that can report information separate from the physical body? I call this part the Inner Self part. Some people call it Higher Self, Inner Self, or Spiritual Self.

Inner Self reports being a part that we are born with, unlike Resource States

that develop over time when the same coping mechanism is used again and again. When I speak directly with the Inner Self part of the client it always speaks with a clear, fearless voice and reports having some knowledge about what the person is here to learn. It will sometimes report being a central part of the person, and it will sometimes report that it is rarely accessed. I do not see inner self as a Resource State. I sometimes access this part intentionally if the client presents with an issue of needing direction in life.

Inner self traits

- It reports having always been with the client.
- It is the one state that everyone appears to have.
- It speaks with a clear, strong, caring voice.
- It claims to have wisdom about the purpose of the person.
- It sometimes reports wishing it was listened to more.
- It can have a low level of energy or a higher level of energy.

9.1.5   Creative Form Identity (CFI)

Creative Form Identities are merely a creative way for Resource States to be represented. These may happen spontaneously or they may be created.

I had a client who was bingeing and who was concerned about his big stomach, as well as his health. I asked to speak to a Resource State that either had some knowledge of the bingeing or was the Resource State that was responsible for the bingeing. I ask that Resource State when it was ready to speak to say, "I'm here." After a small pause I heard a faint, "I'm here."

I thanked the state for speaking to me and asked it if it knew something about the bingeing, or if it caused the bingeing. It replied, "Yes, I do that." I asked again if it was the part that actually caused the bingeing and it replied that it was.

I asked this Resource State, "What name or term fits you? What can I call you?" It replied that I could call it, "Fishy." I commented that that is an interesting name and ask why it wanted me to call it Fishy. It replied that it wanted to be called Fishy because, "I am a fish." I said, "Oh you are. That is interesting. I really want to hear about why you cause the bingeing."

This Resource State that saw itself as a fish told me that it caused the bingeing because it was lonely and that it needed a friend. It said that if it had more room to swim around it might be able to find a friend. It had decided that if the stomach

182

grew bigger it would have a better chance of finding a friend, and then it would not be lonely. It was a Vaded Resource State that held onto the feelings of loneliness.

The mind is amazing and dynamic. I am often struck by how amazing and dynamic it is. This Resource State had learned to identify itself as a fish, possibly because of some fascination with fish as a child, and it was lonely. It is not unusual for Resource States to have needs, like the need for friendship, the need for love, and the need to feel protected.

This 'Fishy' Resource State needed a friend. It was somewhat unusual in that it identified itself as a fish. This is an example of a CFI. It was a Resource State that had developed a creative form identity for itself.

To finish the story about Fishy, I asked him if I were to find him a friend who could play with him if he would stop causing the bingeing. He said, "I guess that would be okay." I then ask to speak with another part who liked to play, and who would enjoy playing with a fish in a nice way. I ask that part to say, "I'm here." A Resource State spoke up and I negotiated the two to be friends and to stay together on the inside. Fishy was happy and the client reported that he stopped bingeing.

Sometimes Resource States are represented as a tightness in the stomach or some other physiological feeling in some part of the body. Sometimes they are represented as the left hand or the right hand. It is not unusual for a person to notice a different psychological feeling on one side or in one part of the body than they feel on the other side or in another part of the body. These are all CFI representations of Resource States.

A CFI is merely a Resource State that is either temporarily or permanently represented in some other form. It recognizes that it is part of the person and in all other ways it is like a Resource State other than its representation in a creative form.

It is sometimes the case that a CFI will see itself as another person. This more often happens if the traits of the Resource State match closely with the traits of the other person, for example a Resource State that shares a lot of traits with 'dad' may say it is 'dad'. This is just another type of creative form identification. The CFI dad is not an Introject, as it is not Resource State specific (different for every

Resource State), and it is not an OPI in that it knows it is part of the person and is where it belongs. These 'other person' CFIs are often manifested in people suffering from Multiple Personality (DID), but they also occasionally appear in other clients.

Traits of CFI's

- They see themselves as part of the person.
- They identify themselves as a part of the body or as some other creative form.
- They are Resource States and are like Resource States in all ways other than their self-identification.
- They have the same kinds of needs that Resource States have and respond in the same way to Resource State interventions.
- They sometimes maintain their creative form identity only temporarily before taking on a normal identity, and they sometimes maintain a creative form identity without taking on a normal identity.

When I speak about a Normal identity for a Resource State I am talking about the Resource State seeing itself as a person of a certain age. A Resource State may see itself as a five-year-old, it may see itself as the age of the person, and occasionally it may see itself as older than the person. Normally, Resource States that see themselves as older than the person do this because they feel tired and rundown. They feel older, therefore they see themselves as older. When a Resource State sees itself as older than the person, or when a Resource State sees itself as the opposite sex from the person it could be considered a CFI.

It is not unusual for Resource States to see themselves as the opposite sex of the person. This usually happens when the traits of a Resource State match the stereotype of the gender. For example, a female who has a Resource State that is very bold and assertive may see this Resource State as male, and the male who has a Resource State that is intuitive or nurturing may identify the state as female. It is more common for individuals to see all of their Resource States as the same gender that they are, but there it is not an issue if individuals have Resource States that identify themselves as the opposite sex of the person.

9.1.6 Other Personalized Introject (OPI)

There are two types of Introjects, internalized impressions held by Resource States, and the much more rare, Other Personalized Introjects (OPIs). The personality is dynamic and fascinating, as evidenced by the occasional presentation of an OPI. OPIs are occasional expressions that, 1) claim not to be a part of the person and, 2) say they are not where they belong.

When spoken with directly they will claim to not be a part of the personality, and unlike Resource States they can permanently leave the personality. While their etiology is unclear, I find when they are negotiated with to leave they can do so without any further indication of being present. Clients show improvement and often say they feel physically lighter.

The precise negotiation process to achieve this improvement uses imagery to assist the OPI to go to a light. I chose the imagery of a light because most cultures have an archetypal conceptualization of 'the light' as being a positive destination. I suggest to the OPI that while I understand it may not feel it can go to the light, it actually can. It just cannot take anything heavy or negative with it.

I suggest to the OPI that it does not have to do anything that it does not want to do, and that we can just explore what its possibilities are, so it can make up its own mind.

I use the RT Action 14, The Separation Sieve, to allow the OPI to experience what it feels like after it leaves everything heavy or negative in the sieve. Then I invite the OPI to visit the light, so it can make up its own mind. I suggest to it that if it wants to help the client it can help much more from the light.

This process is completely non-coercive, and upon visiting the light and hearing that it can help as much as it chooses from there, it wants to stay. After an OPI has left, regardless of timeframe, other Resource States will consistently report, 'It left.' This is normally a short negotiation, and one that can be very beneficial for the client.

Identifying OPIs

When an OPI is asked, "Are you part of this person?" it will respond with something like, "No, I'm not part of her." OPIs speak about the client in the third person, "She will never amount to anything." While some Resource States will speak about other Resource States in the third person, "I don't like that part," there is normally an acknowledgment that the two Resource States are different parts of the same person. When talking with an OPI there is an impression that you are almost talking with someone else, and not the client.

OPIs will often say things like, "I know I shouldn't be here." "You can't make me leave," or "I am afraid to go." Sometimes OPIs will even claim to be another person who has died.

When an OPI is negotiated to leave, the client will often report that a very critical voice that may have been heard for years is no longer heard. After an OPI has been negotiated with to leave I have never had the client come back to me and say that they wish it was there again. Following the OPI negotiation, there is a very positive and good feeling. There is real therapeutic value.

There is a fundamental difference between an OPI and a Resource State. A Resource State is a physiological part of the person and it cannot leave. It is part of the brain, a neural pathway. It is possible to ask a Resource State to leave and it may agree to do so, but the next time the client is hypnotized if you asked to talk to that Resource State, it is immediately there and able to talk. Therefore, it appears that Resource States do not leave, and cannot leave, but may sometimes step into the background. When an OPI leaves and later if you ask to speak with that OPI a Resource State will speak up and say something like, "He's not here. He left." It is very clear that OPIs can leave, and when they do they are no longer available for conversation.

OPIs could be looked at as an unknown manifestation of the dynamic brain. The personality is truly fascinating. OPIs will sometimes report reasons why they are there. They often will say, "Don't make me leave. I don't want to die." They occasionally report being a relative or friend of the person to whom I am talking. They sometimes report the sense of being lost, and they sometimes report that they are needed to be with this person, often to be critical of them, 'to keep them in line'. They sometimes share the belief that if they go they will die, or that they can't go where they should, 'Into the light,' because they are not good enough to be there.

They are often, although not always, negative and they often express being confused. They are sometimes gruff and highly critical. Very occasionally they can appear malevolent.

I have found that almost all OPIs report being there because they fear moving on, or do not believe they belong in the light. Sometimes they report being there to "Keep her in line." In the more rare instances of OPIs reporting that they do not want to leave a loved one, I tell them than they can go to the light and then still guide their loved one from the light. I tell them that it is their being stuck that causes the client to feel heavy. Being free to move to the light does not mean a separation. I tell them that the loving connection can be stronger when there is no fear. They are then able to leave.

Traits of OPIs

- They report that they are not part of the person.
- The same OPI can be seen the same by a number of different Resource States, unlike Introjects that are interpreted differently by each Resource State. Each Resource State has its own Introjects.
- They report that they are not where they should be.
- They usually report feeling unable to move to where they should be.
- They are often a very critical voice inside the person. (It is also possible for a Resource State to be a critical voice.)
- When it is made clear that they can move to where they should be, but they just cannot take negativity with them, they become less resistant.
- They can leave and afterward Resource States continue to report that they are no longer present.
- When they move to 'where the light is' they become euphoric and happy to stay with the light, and this leaves the person feeling physically lighter and with a sense of being more free to be themselves.

It is impossible to interpret with complete understanding all the different things that are manifested in the personality.

9.1.7 Action 14 The Separation Sieve

Purpose: The Separation Sieve Action is a very useful therapeutic mechanism that facilitates the client to use the metaphor of going through a sieve, in order to focus readiness and intent to accept change. This Action can be used to assist clients in letting go of guilt, letting go of connections to a past partner, or letting go of trauma.

When should it be used? This Action is most useful when the client is having difficulty letting go of guilt, shame, anger, trauma, or an unwanted connection to another person. It is important that the correct Resource be in the Conscious when this Action is used. For example, when this Action is employed to facilitate the client to release feelings of guilt, it is important that the Resource that has those feelings of guilt be in the Conscious.

Process: The Separation Sieve Action is not difficult, and it is composed of 10 straightforward steps.

The steps will be listed below and then further explained.

1. Make sure the correct Resource is in the Conscious.
2. Check to see if the client is ready to experiment in letting go.
3. Describe the sieve.
4. Describe coming through the sieve leaving everything negative behind.
5. Ask the Resource how it is feeling.
6. Ask the Resource to look back up in the sieve and described what that stuff looks like that was left behind.
7. Ask the Resource if it wants any of that stuff back.
8. Asked the Resource what color of light, or fluid, would sizzle that stuff completely away.
9. Provide the image of the stuff in the sieve sizzling away with the light or fluid.
10. Ask the Resource how it feels now.

Step 1: Make sure the correct Resource is in the Conscious.

The first step in the Separation Sieve Action is to ensure that the correct Resource is in the Conscious. Most often, when this Action is employed the therapist will be aware that the correct Resource is already in the Conscious, because that Resource will be expressing an unwanted emotional reaction relating to something such as guilt that the client would like to release. If the correct Resource is not already in the Conscious the Vivify Specific Action (see Action 2) can be used to make sure the correct Resource is out.

Step 2: Check to see if the client is ready to experiment in letting go.

It is important to check on the readiness of the client to let go, e.g., of something like guilt, or the connection to a lost relationship. This may be obvious. It may be the reason the client has come to therapy, but sometimes the client may not be fully ready to let go. If this is the case the Sieve Action may be introduced as an exploration to help the client determine if he or she wants to let go. Therefore, it is not important if the client is sure about letting go. The Sieve Action can be used to help the client determine this.

Step 3: Describe the sieve.

Ensure that the client's eyes are closed. This can be done by saying, "Just allow your eyes to close right now." When the client's eyes are closed the image of the sieve can be constructed.

Example: "Just allow your eyes to close. There is a very powerful magic sieve. It is much more powerful than it needs to be. Nothing heavy, dark, sticky or negative can possibly come through the sieve, only lightness. You can come through the sieve but nothing heavy can possibly come through. No guilt, shame, anger, regret, or unwanted connections can possibly come through this sieve. Just as an experiment you will be able to come easily through the sieve down to where my voice is, then you will be able to decide if there is anything that was caught in the sieve that you want back."

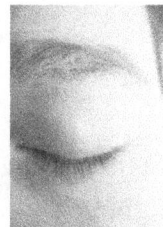

Step 4: Describe coming through and leaving everything heavy behind.

"This is just an experiment, so you can fall through the sieve and then make your decision. So right now just allow the light you, the free you, the pure essence of you, to fall directly through the sieve down to where my voice is, leaving anything heavy or sticky or negative behind. Come straight through now to where my voice is."

Step 5: Ask the Resource how it is feeling.

"How does that feel?"

Step 6: Ask the Resource to look back up at the sieve and describe what the stuff that was left behind looks like.

"Look back up at the sieve and tell me what the stuff that is caught in it looks like."

Step 7: Ask the Resource if it wants any of that stuff back.

"Do you want any of that back?"

Step 8: Ask the Resource what color of light, or fluid, would sizzle that stuff completely away.

"What color of light or fluid, would sizzle that stuff away, into complete nothingness?"

(If the Resource responds with only a color and does not say if it is a light or fluid, ask, "Is that a light or a fluid.")

Step 9: Provide the image of the stuff in the sieve sizzling away with the light or fluid.

(E.g., If the client answers, 'A blue light'.) "Okay, let's just allow that blue light, much more powerful than it needs to be, to go straight through the sieve sizzling all of that stuff completely away. Czzzzzzzzz, completely away, Czzzzzzzzzzzz."

Step 10: Ask the Resource how it feels now.

"How do you feel now?"

The client may now be told, "It is alright to just go ahead and allow your eyes to open so we can talk about this further."

After coming through the image of the sieve it is very unusual for a resource to say they want any of the stuff in the sieve back. Normally, when asked if they want any of that stuff back the response a definite, "No, I don't want any of THAT back." If there is an exception to this a negotiation can be conducted to allow something that the client wants to keep to come through the sieve in a transformed, positive and beautiful form. What is unwanted, can be sizzled away. Following this process clients will often say they feel lighter.

Obviously, there is no three-dimensional sieve that separates clients from their unwanted baggage. The imagery metaphor of the sieve allows the client to focus intent in a safe way. Clients understand that this is an experiment, and they will be able to have anything back the way it was, if they choose. This experiment allows the client to experience what it feels like to let go of emotionally heavy feelings.

9.1.8   OPI Intervention

Over the years I have developed techniques for negotiating with OPIs so the client can feel lighter and relieved. I have found it does not matter what the client thinks about OPIs, and I do not try to convince the client to think about them in any way. After the therapy, I merely ask, "How are you feeling now?" and how the client reports is what is important to me.

Here is how I negotiate with OPIs to leave. As stated above, there appears to be an archetypal impression of going to a white light where there are loved ones waiting, where there is an unconditional love, and where there is peace. Interestingly, when I ask an OPI how they feel about going to the light I have never gotten a question, "What is that?" There has been an implicit understanding of the light as being a place where some people go. This underlines the cross-cultural acceptance of this archetype.

First, I establish that I am speaking with an OPI, that is, a part that says that it is not part of the person, a part that sees the person as someone else, and a part that recognizes that it is not where it should be.

OPIs are often nervous about speaking with me, because they are afraid I will make them go someplace else and they are afraid of what that might be like. Therefore, I tell the OPI that I am not going to make them do anything. I tell them that anything that they do is going to be totally up to them, and I also say that, "I know that it seems like you are not able to go to the light, but you will be able to." They often, at first, have difficulty accepting this.

OPIs, generally, see themselves as 'not good enough' to go to the light. They think they would not be welcome there, and that they would not fit in. Therefore, I tell them that it is true that they cannot take their negativity with them, they cannot take their dark, heavy anger and resentment and jealousy with them, but that they can go to the light. I tell them that we can do an experiment so they can see, then if they want everything back like it was they can have it that way. I have found it is important that they not feel pushed or coerced.

I tell them that there is a magical sieve that we will use (This is the Separation Sieve, Action 14). I tell them that only the part of them that can go to the light will be able to pass through the sieve and that the sieve will collect all the negativity, all the dark sticky, heavy bits, and it is totally impossible for that stuff to go through the sieve. I tell them that the sieve is much more powerful than it needs to be so passing through will be like dropping off a heavy coat and leaving it in the sieve.

I tell them that they can now allow themselves to fall straight through the sieve and feel what it is like to be only the part of them that can go to the light. I then ask them to look back up at the sieve and tell me what that stuff in the sieve looks like. They normally say it is dark and heavy and they often say it looks sticky. I then ask them, "Do you want any of that back?" They always say that they do not want anything back from the sieve. They are emphatic about that.

I then ask what color of light or fluid would sizzle that stuff in the sieve into nothingness. When they tell me a color I then ask, "Is that a light or is that a fluid." When they tell me, then I say let's just have that, for example, purple light sizzle straight through the sieve and sizzle that stuff into complete nothingness, and I make a sizzling noise.

192

Then I say something like, "Now, there is someone who loves you that is pulling you like a magnet to come to the light to where they are waiting." I tell them to just allow yourself to feel the pull and to go on and explore what it is like there in the light. I tell them to just go for a visit and see what they want to do. I tell them to just allow themselves to be drawn into that complete unconditional love by that magnetic pull.

The voice of the OPI becomes very soft, relaxed, and even sometimes euphoric. I then tell the OPI that it can stay there where the light is if it wants to, and I ask it if that is what it would like to do. It is very happy to stay. I tell it, that is fine, and tell it that it is good that it will be able to enjoy where it now is.

I pause for a few seconds, and then I address the client directly by name, and ask something like, "How are you feeling now?" Practically without exception, the client reports feeling physically lighter.

This work feels like some of the best work I do. Before I started working in this way with clients who manifested this negative, "I am not part of her" part, were very slow to progress, and then it was often limited progress. Following up with clients after their OPI leaves, I have received feedback from, "I have not really noticed much difference," to, "My whole life has changed. The loud critical voice on the inside is no longer there and I feel so much better, lighter and more able to be myself."

9.2 Skills for Day 9

9.2.1 Practice: Using the Separation Sieve

1. Suggest there is a powerful sieve that cannot possibly let anything heavy through.

2. Just as an experiment (everything can be returned to as it was if wanted) the state can easily come through to 'where my voice is', dropping anything heavy, like a heavy coat sliding off.

3. Ask how that feels now.

4. Ask the state to look back up at the sieve and tell what that stuff looks like.

5. Ask if it wants any of that back.

6. Ask what color of light or fluid would sizzle it into nothingness.

7. Make a sizzling noise and indicate it is all gone.

9.3 Quiz and Activities for Day 9

9.3.1 Quiz

1. What is an Introject?

2. What is a Resource State?

3. What is an OPI?

4. What is a CFI?

5. Why is it important to present the use of the Separation Sieve as, just an experiment?

6. How can the Separation Sieve be used to reduce guilt?

7. How can the Separation Sieve the used as an alternative to bridging and Vaded State resolution?

8. What is the state sometimes referred to as Inner Self?

9. How can Inner Self sometimes be used in Therapy?

10. How does a client normally report feeling following an OPI leaving?

9.3.2 Activity

Fill in the following table with either, Resource, Introject, Inner Self, CFI, or OPI

1.	It is the one state that everyone appears to have.	
2.	It is a physiological part of the brain.	

3. When we bridge we always go to one of them.	
4. They report that they are not part of the person.	
5. It speaks with a clear, strong, caring voice.	
6. They report that they are not where they should be.	
7. We can feel an inner peace when they respect each other and get along.	
8. They are created by a Resource State when it takes on an internalized impression.	
9. They are created by repetition usually in childhood.	
10. It claims to have wisdom about the purpose of the person.	
11. They are Resource States and are like Resource States in all ways other than their self-identification.	
12. They identify themselves as a part of the body or as some other creative form.	
13. They can leave and afterward Resource States continue to report that they are no longer present.	
14. A Vaded Resource State is vaded because of the impressions it holds about these.	
15. They cannot be destroyed and they cannot leave.	
16. They can slightly change their role, and they can change the amount they come out.	

10 Day 10 Review and Anchoring

Day 10 is a lighter day of training, as it is the last day. It has a review of the major aspects of the therapy so you are able to refresh in any area that may need fuller understanding.

Action 15, Anchoring is also covered. This is a very useful technique to help clients bring preferred states to the Conscious. Some clients are interested in bringing forth their best sporting states, their best speaking states, or even their best states to relax or sleep. With the help of an anchor, and with pathology addressed, clients should be able to bring out their most preferred state whenever they choose. This is very empowering, and enjoyable. When a rest state can identify as being a relaxing cat (CFI), and feel that experience, it allows that state to more easily become the Conscious state.

A short definition of the day ten terms is provided below. You should make sure you are comfortable with the fuller meaning of these terms by the end of this final day's training.

10.1 Core Concepts for Day 10 Training

Page #'s are Hyperlinks on eBooks		Page
Vaded with Fear	A state that is carrying unresolved fear from an ISE.	199
Vaded with Rejection	A state that feels unlovable or unworthy.	199
Vaded with Confusion	A state that cannot stop ruminating about something. Sometimes guilt, shame, or blame.	199

10.1 Core Concepts for Day 10 Training		
Vaded with Disappointment	A sad feeling state that is so disappointed it blocks other states from positive activity. This state causes psychological depression.	200
Retro Original	An unwanted behavior that was learned in childhood while the state was forming.	200
Retro Avoiding	An unwanted behavior actioned to help avoid the bad feelings of a state Vaded with Fear or Rejection.	200
Conflicted	A state that does not appreciate another state and is in conflict with it.	201
Dissonant	A healthy state that is conscious at the wrong time. It often feels incompetent.	201
Action 15 Anchoring	A technique to help clients bring out a preferred state.	201
Common Supervision Issues	Issues most often needing more focus and understanding.	203

10.1.1   Vaded with Fear

How is a Resource Vaded with Fear Pathological?	Normal State
A Resource Vaded with Fear is stuck in a past event. It actually believes it is still happening. When it comes to the surface it brings with it fear that interferes with the ability of the client to respond to life's current challenges.	Normal States hold no fear from the past. They can appropriately fear something present that could hurt them, but they no longer harbor fear from events that come from the past. They are able to make wise decisions based on current realities.

10.1.2   Vaded with Rejection

How is a Resource Vaded with Rejection Pathological?	Normal State
A Resource Vaded with Rejection believes it is unlovable, or not good enough. This can keep the client from engaging, and can cause the client to question personal value or to over compete.	Normal States have positive feelings about themselves. They enjoy the time they have in the Conscious and feel they have something to offer.

10.1.3   Vaded with Confusion

How is a Resource Vaded with Confusion Pathological?	Normal State
A Resource Vaded with Confusion cannot let something go. It ruminates to the point of obsession. The client cannot settle, sometimes for months or years.	Normal States can accept things as they are. There may be hard times, but Normal States can let hard times go within a reasonable timeframe.

10.1.4   Vaded with Disappointment

How is a Resource Vaded with Disappointment Pathological?	Normal State
A Resource Vaded with Disappointment carries a level of sorrow, which 1) causes it to feel upset, and 2) causes it to not want other Resource States to feel happy. It blocks energy from the personality.	Normal States feel good about what they do, and they are happy when other Normal States also help the personality.

10.1.5   Retro Original

How is a Retro Original State Pathological?	Normal State
A Retro Original State carries out behavior learned in childhood that becomes unwanted by other personality states. This causes the client to feel regret and a lack of personal control.	Normal States carry out behavior that other states appreciate. Normal states feel at peace with each other.

10.1.6   Retro Avoiding

How is a Retro Avoiding State Pathological?	Normal State
A Retro Avoiding State carries out (addictive) behavior unwanted by other states so the personality does not have to experience the anxiety of a Vaded State.	Normal States carry out behavior that other states appreciate. Normal states feel at peace with each other.

10.1.7 Conflicted

How are Conflicted States Pathological?	Normal State
Conflicted States cause anxiety because they do not respect and understand each other. They each want different things and they hold negative feelings about the state with which they are conflicted.	Normal States respect each other and they feel thankful that other Normal States are there to do the things they do not want to do, or do not have the abilities to do.

10.1.8 Dissonant

How are Dissonant States Pathological?	Normal State
Dissonant States can cause the client to feel like performance is below par, can cause the client to feel like, 'I know I can do better', or can cause the client to feel frustrated with self.	When a Normal State is Conscious it feels like it is the best part to be out. It feels good to hold the Conscious and feels like it has the opportunity to make a contribution.

10.1.9 Action 15 Anchoring

Anchoring is a useful technique that can assist the client to bring into the Conscious the preferred Resource State. For example, a person participating in a sport may want to bring into the Conscious the Resource that can best play that sport. A person taking an exam may want to bring into the Conscious the Resource State that studied. A person wanting to relax may want to bring into the Conscious a Resource that is good at relaxing.

Clients can become better at bringing out the best Resource State by learning a mnemonic memory technique. They are trained to associate a particular animal with the state they want to bring to the Conscious. By focusing on the experience of their chosen animal, they are better able to gain access to their preferred Resource State.

Clients will be able to bring their preferred Resource State into the Conscious as long as a Vaded State is not forcing its way into the Conscious, or as long as a Vaded State is not actively being avoided by a Retro Avoiding State. In other words, in order to be able to bring out the preferred Resource it is important that any related Vaded States first be resolved. It is easy to understand this by considering a person who has of phobia about spiders. It is impossible for this person to decide, "I just want to be relaxed now," before the Vaded State that underpins the fear is resolved. Until it is resolved it will overpower the ability of the client to bring out the preferred Resource State.

Therefore, if a Vaded State is part of the issue, Anchoring is a technique that is only useful after the Vaded State resolution. If a Dissonant state is the issue, no Vaded State resolution is necessary.

Here is an example of when it would be most appropriate to use Anchoring. A client presents due to the fear of public speaking. If the client describes a high level of anxiety when attempting to speak publicly, then a Vaded State is involved. RT Actions 2 to 7 can be used to resolve the negative feelings of the Vaded State. Next, a Resource State that enjoys communicating can be found using RT Action 8, Find Resource, and this Resource State can be given a name. The client will be wanting to bring this communicative Resource State out whenever any slight anxiety is felt while communicating in front of a group. The Anchoring technique will assist the client in being able to bring out the communicative Resource State.

The Anchoring technique can also be used to assist clients to bring out Resource States when Vaded States have not been involved (Dissonant State involvement). Examples of this include test taking (often a nervous Resource State assumes the Conscious when the client would prefer the Resource State that studied) and sport participation (a Resource State that is concerned about performance may hold the Conscious, rather than a Resource State that participates well). Even in these instances if the client reports experiencing exaggerated levels of emotion, then a Vaded State will need to be resolved prior to using the Anchoring technique.

Anchoring and the 3 other RT Actions it entails

1. The **Vivify Specific Action** is used to vivify a time when the client wants to bring in a preferred state. This will bring to the Conscious the state that has not been preferred. If it is emotional it is Vaded, and if it just feels uncomfortable or incompetent it is Dissonant.

2. Next, the **Find Resource Action** is used in order to find the preferred state.

   Once the preferred state is found, and named, that state is asked what type of animal it most associates with itself.

   It is asked to describe the animal in some detail, to describe its breathing, to describe the setting that it is in, and to describe what it feels like being this animal. The animal becomes the anchor.

3. Finally, the **Imagery Check Action** is used to allow the client to practice remembering the feeling of the animal within the image whenever the associated Resource State is desired.

In *Resource Therapy* (Emmerson, 2014), Anchoring is illustrated with the example of a client wanting to improve sporting performance.

10.1.10 Common Supervision Topics

This section relates to some of the issues brought up during supervision sessions with Resource Therapists. I supervise a number of therapists who have studied Resource Therapy. There are some common issues they bring to supervision that may be beneficial to address here.

Bridging

Therapist: I am having trouble bridging. I'm not sure I'm getting to the initial sensitizing event.

Supervisor: Tell me exactly what you say during the bridging process. What exactly do you say to clients?

Therapist: I tell them to go to the first time they remember having this feeling.

Supervisor: When you use the word remember, you are asking the client to intellectually remember something. That is taking the client away from their Vaded State, into an intellectual state. The only way they will be able to bridge is by having their Vaded State in the Conscious. It is the feelings of the Vaded State that allows that state to connect with the event that caused those feelings. Make sure, while you are bridging, that you only ask about experiences and feelings. Never ask the client to remember, think back, or think about when was the first time you experienced this? It is impossible to bridge unless the client is in the Vaded State.

Therapist: When should I bridge?

Supervisor: You should bridge when the client has a State Vaded with Fear or Rejection. There are other techniques for helping clients with the other types of pathological Resource States.

Changing Chairs Introject Action

Therapist: I wanted to use the Changing Chairs Introject Action, and my client was not comfortable with that. She felt silly talking to an empty chair.

Supervisor: How did you introduce that Action to her?

Therapist: I told her there was an activity I would like to try. I asked her if she would be comfortable talking to an empty chair, pretending that her husband was there?

Supervisor: You are the professional therapist. The client has come to you for your professional understanding of techniques, and for you to select the techniques that will help her get the change that she desires. It will be easier for the client when you tell her clearly the steps you want her to follow. If a person goes to a medical doctor with a wound filled with dirt the doctor will not ask the client if the client thinks that wound should be cleaned out and scrubbed, or left the way it is. The medical doctor knows that the wound should be cleaned and gives the client clear instructions so that the wound can be cleaned. In the same way, if you see that the Changing Chairs Introject Activity will help your client become less confused, it is better not to put the responsibility of which technique to use onto the client. Merely pull an empty chair in front of the client, and clearly say, 'This is what I want you to do.' The client will follow your clear instructions, will not be stressed about having to make a therapeutic decision, and will benefit from your professional knowledge.

Holding a State in the Conscious

Therapist: I am having trouble holding the emotional state in the Conscious. I can get the state into the conscious using the Vivify Specific Action, but then it seems like another state takes over.

Supervisor: As soon as you get a Resource State into the Conscious it is important to get a name for it, and continue to call it by that name. If you use its name constantly, almost in every sentence, it will stay in the conscious. It is also helpful to think about talking directly to that state. When states are addressed directly they continue to stay in the Conscious. An example is, if someone sees you a bit emotional, and if they make a statement recognizing your emotions, that will bring that emotional state into the Conscious. It has been spoken to.

Therapist: What is the best way to ask a Resource State to name itself?

Supervisor: It is better not to say, 'What can I call this part of you?' When you recognize the state that you want to speak with is in the Conscious, say, 'What can I call you, this part that (e.g., is feeling upset)'. Imagine being in a room full of people and wanting to know the person's name you are speaking with. You would not say to that person, 'What can I call this person I'm talking with?' You would say, 'What can I call you? It is always important to speak directly to a Resource State as if you are talking to an individual. That will help it stay in the Conscious, and that will help it feel respected.

Vivify Specific

Therapist: I'm not sure I'm getting the right Resource State into the Conscious in order to do therapeutic work. The Vivify Specific Action does not seem to be working for me.

Supervisor: Tell me exactly what you are saying to the client.

Therapist: I tell him to tell me about a time he felt upset.

Supervisor: That sounds good. Then what happens?

Therapist: He tells me he feels upset most at work. But it seems like he stays in an intellectual Resource State.

Supervisor: Are you making sure he tells you about one specific instance when he felt upset at work?

Therapist: Probably not. He just tells me he feels upset at work.

Supervisor: That is an intellectual state telling about the problem. That is not the state that actually experiences the problem. In order to gain access to the state that actually experiences the problem you have to get him to tell you about a specific instance, and then have him to tell more about that instance in detail, while you speak with him in the first person tense.

Therapist: What do you mean the first person tense?

Supervisor: It is not the first person tense if you say to him, 'What was the expression on your boss's face?' It is the first person tense if you say to him, 'Right now, sitting at your desk, in the middle of the afternoon, what is your boss looking like, as he is looking at you?' In order to Vivify Specific, you must first have the client describe in detail one specific incident, and you must begin to talk with the client about being inside that incident using first person tense. It is much easier to do this when you ask clients to allow their eyes to close, as soon as you are able to get the one, specific incident that you want to vivify. Clients are better able to connect with an event with their eyes closed, because they are not having to process all the visual information currently in front of them.

Therapist: When do I know they are in the right Resource State?

Supervisor: You will be able to recognize that. There's a big difference between talking with an intellectual state about something, and with talking to the state that is emotional. It is clear when a nervous Resource State comes into the Conscious.

Duck Billed Platypus Therapy

Therapist: Sometimes it seems like this just isn't going to go anywhere. I get lost and I don't know what to do next.

Supervisor: Yes, that happens to me too. I practice what I called the Duck Billed Platypus form of therapy.

Therapist: What's that?

Supervisor: A Duck Billed Platypus swims underwater with its eyes closed. When it bumps into a rock it backs up, moves over to the side, and goes forward again. If it bumps into the rock a second time, it backs up, moves over again, and goes forward. It continues to do this until he gets around the rock. If I try something in therapy and it doesn't work, I remember what the client is ready to change, I back up a bit, move over, and try something else. That does not mean I will get around every rock, but it does help me in working with clients.

Highly emotional clients

Therapist: When I bridged my client became so emotional she said she did not want to continue.

Supervisor: It is understandable that clients will become emotional. That is often why they are coming to therapy. When we work with the client to bridge to an emotional initial sensitizing event, it is especially understandable that they may feel unable to handle the situation. That is why it is something that is bothering them currently. Because we know it is only an illusion, an Introject from the past, that is problematic for them we can show strength and understanding. This will help them become empowered. If, after bridging, the client says to me, 'I can't do this,' I will say something like, 'That's OK. We don't have to. Since we know this isn't happening now, if you could do this, what kind of thing would you have liked to have said?' Another thing I might say is, 'That's fine. We don't have to. Let's just shrink him down to 1 inch tall. He is tiny with a squeaky little voice. Please don't step on him, because I want you to be able to tell him what you want to say.' The key is to help the client feel comfortable. Do not tell the client, "We have to do something that you don't want to do." Tell the client it is fine not to continue, but then help the client understand that all the power is held by the Resource State.

> **Key** It is much better to leave a Resource State feeling empowered, expressed, understood, protected, and cared for, than to back out and leave the Resource State holding the same fear that it has felt for years.

Introducing Resource Therapy to Clients

Therapist: How do I introduce Resource Therapy to my clients?

Supervisor: When I have a new client, I merely say that the personality is composed of parts; part of me might want to do one thing while another part might like to do something else. I say that I work to make sure that I speak directly with the part that needs change. Then I ask if there are any questions. Actually, very few clients have questions following this introduction, but if they do I merely answer them.

Information about books, Resource Therapists, and training can be found at ResourceTherapy.com

10.2 Skills for Day 10

10.2.1 Practice: Dissonant States using Anchors

1. Locate a state that is a less preferred state to be Conscious at a time.

2. Ask the client how he or she would like both to feel and act at that time.

3. Ask when the client has had that experience in the past and vivify that time.

4. Get a name for that state and ask it if it will help at the needed time.

5. Get permission from the Dissonant State and have it to speak directly to the other state asking it for help.

6. Ask the preferred state what animal it associates with itself and vivify that animal in the location the client visualizes it.

7. Suggest that anytime the client wants to bring out the preferred state to think about the animal in the place where it was visualized.

8. Imagery Check.

10.3 Quiz and Activities for Day 10 Training

10.3.1 Quiz

1. What type of pathological state is most likely involved in writers block?

2. What type of pathological state is most likely involved in a sporting slump?

3. How do you tell the difference in a Dissonant State and a Vaded State?

4. If a client reports being highly emotional when attempting to talk in front of a group what type of pathological state is likely involved?

5. If a client reports being uncomfortable and unable to think clearly when attempting to talk in front of a group what type of pathological state is likely involved?

6. What is the name of the international Resource Therapy organization?

7. Who gets to have a name listed in the international Resource Therapy organization database, as a qualified clinical Resource Therapist?

8. What is a therapeutic anchor?

9. Why is it important to vivify the client as an animal in order to bring out a preferred Resource state?

10. What is the best animal for a client to select?

10.3.2 Day 10 Crossword

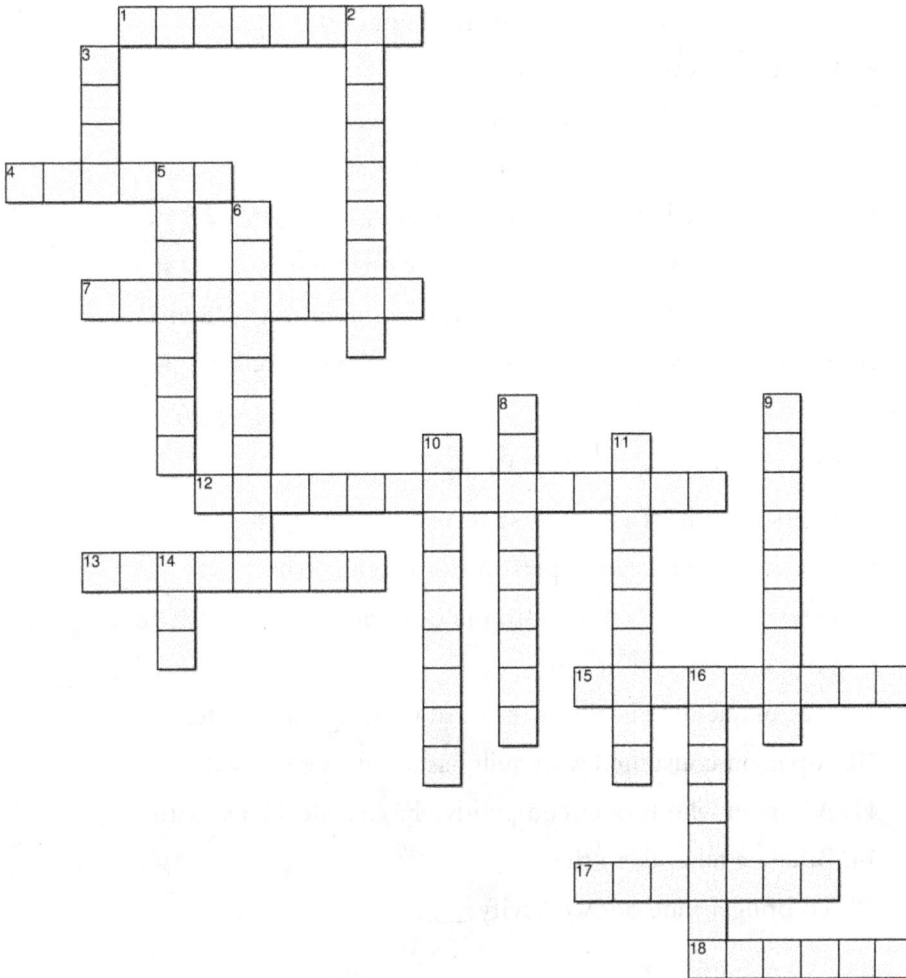

Across

- 1. An unwanted behavior learned in childhood is Retro
- 4. A state is a healthy condition is
- 7. Most Fear and Rejection Vaded states were vaded in ____.
- 12. A person with depression has a state Vaded with
- 13. When a state is Vaded with Fear or Rejection we use__ to get to ISE.
- 15. When a less preferred state is Conscious there is a ____ state.
- 17. A state that often comes into the Conscious is a __ State.
- 18. What is switched during the Changing Chairs Action?

Down

- 2. When most states are Vaded with Confusion.
- 3. A person with PTSD has a state Vaded with ____.
- 5. A behavior that keeps a person from feeling bad
- 6. A state that rarely comes into the Conscious is an ____ State.
- 8. When a state is out it is ____.
- 9. A technique to help the client learn to bring out a state.
- 10. A person consumed with guilt has a state Vaded with
- 11. A person who is over competitive has a state Vaded with ____.
- 14. Bridging takes us to the ____.
- 16. To bring a state out we Vivify ____.

Recognition of Prior Learning (RPL)

Students who complete a 10 day training with a Resource Therapy International approved trainer gain a Clinical Qualification in Resource Therapy. RPL credit may be gained from the study of this manual according to the following guidelines.

1. RT trainers may, at their discretion, grant a reduced fee for a demonstrated level of proficiency* gained from the study of this manual.
2. Trainers may grant credit for up to the first two days of training for a demonstrated level of proficiency* gained from study of this manual.
3. Any additional level/s of RPL may only be granted by Resource Therapy International.
4. The application process for this is through direct application to the President of RTI. See www.ResourceTherapyInternational.com

See ResourceTherapyInternational.com for a list of approved RT Trainers.

*An appropriate level of proficiency may be demonstrated during an interview where core RT concepts are discussed.

11 Appendix 1 Daily Activity Answers

11.1 Day 1 Answers

Quiz (with answers) Day 1

1. **Q. What is the purpose of the Vivify Specific Action?**

- **A.** This is the action that is used to bring the preferred Resource State into the Conscious. This action is needed in practically all Resource Therapy work, as the power of the therapy has to do with working with the state that needs assistance.

2. **Q. What is the purpose of Bridging?**

- **A.** Bridging is used when there is a state Vaded with rejection or fear, in order to find the ISE. The state Vaded with rejection or fear needs to become empowered in the image of the ISE so that the feeling of rejection or fear can be replaced by calmness and support.

3. **Q. What is the difference between Surface and Underlying States?**

- **A.** Surface States are out often during daily routine. Underlying States more often childhood states and rarely come out into the Conscious. It is often Underlying States that have been Vaded with fear or rejection. It is often Surface States that are Vaded with confusion or disappointment.

4. **Q. Where do Resource States come from?**

- **A.** Resource States are a physiological part of the brain. They grow with axon and dendrite development mainly during childhood. Trained synaptic firings and axon and dendrite growth form Resource States due to repetition of coping skills. They are us.

5. **Q. What are Introjects?**

- **A.** Introjects are our internalized impressions that Resource States hold. Each Resource State will have its own Introjects of other people. A childhood Resource State may have an Introject of dad as being demanding, while an adult Resource State may have an Introject of dad as being helpful.

6. **Q. What are pathological states called that have unwanted feelings?**
- **A.** Vaded States

7. **Q. What are pathological states called that do unwanted behaviors?**
- **A.** Retro States

8. **Q. What are pathological states called that are in conflict with other states to the point of anxiety?**
- **A.** Conflicted States

9. **Q. What are states called that prefer not to be out when they are, and wish another state would take over?**
- **A.** Dissonant States

10. **Q. What does it mean to talk in the present tense?**
- **A.** Talking in the present tense means using words such as is, and are, and demanding that the client also speak about what is happening, rather than what did happen.

Day 1 Crossword Answers

<u>Down</u>

- 1. Original Nationality of Helen Watkins /German
- 2. RT Techniques to help Clients /Actions
- 3. Emotionally upset States /Vaded
- 4. They started Ego State Therapy /Watkins
- 5. Helpful to know ___ of State at ISE to Bridge /Age
- 7. Retro State that learned behavior in Childhood /Original
- 9. Personality Parts /Resources
- 10. Resources rarely in the Conscious 9,6 /Underlying States
- 11. What a depressed state is Vaded with /Disappointment
- 14. Action to go from an emotion to the ISE /Briding
- 15. A student of Federn and teacher of Watkins /Weiss
- 18. What a ruminating state is Vaded with Confusion
- 19. What a state that feels unlovable is Vaded with /Rejection
- 20. Two States that are fighting each other /Conflicted
- 22. What a state with a phobia is Vaded with /Fear

- 24. Retro State that causes addictions /Avoiding
- 26. Trains client to bring preferred state out /Anchoring
- 27. He first conceived personality states /Federn

Across

- 5. Personality Parts for Multiple Personality /Alters
- 6. Unwanted Behavior /Retro
- 8. Founder of Resource Therapy /Emmerson
- 11. Multiple Personality's current designation /DID
- 12. Nationality of Edoardo Weiss /Italian
- 13. Usual time states can be Vaded with Confusion /Adulthood
- 16. Nationality of Paul Federn /Austrian
- 17. Nationality of John Watkins /American
- 21. Action for therapist to bring wanted state into Conscious 6,8 /Vivify Specific
- 23. Resources used Daily 7,6 /Surface States
- 25. Nationality of Gordon Emmerson /Australian
- 28. Internalized Impressions /Introjects
- 29. Usual time states can be Vaded with Rejection /Childhood
- 30. Wrong Resource State in the Conscious /Dissonant
- 31. When a state is out and in control /Conscious
- 32. Healthy Resource States Normal

11.2 Day 2 Answers

1. Q. When did states Vaded with Fear and Rejection normally become Vaded?

- **A.** Childhood

2. Q. How should a therapist introduce working with empty chairs?

- **A.** The therapist should merely pull a chair out and instruct the client in terms of what the therapist wants a client to do. The therapist should not ask the client for permission to do good therapeutic work.

3. Q. What if the client talks about the person in the other chair, rather than to that person?

- **A.** It is imperative that the therapist have the client speak directly to the person in the other chair. If the client says, "I would like him to know that," the therapist needs to say, call him by name and say that directly to him.

4. Q. What is the Expression Action used for?

- **A.** The expression Action is the most empowering action for working with states Vaded with fear or rejection. When a Vaded State learns that it can say absolutely anything and be safe it learns that the Introject that it once feared or felt rejected by has no power in the present.

5. Q. When should the Introject Speak Action be used?

- **A.** The Introject speak action is used to enable a state Vaded with rejection to gain the understanding that the rejecting person was not good at showing unconditional love. This understanding allows the state Vaded with rejection to realize it was not that state that was unlovable; it was the other person who was unable to show unconditional love.

6. Q. During which Action may a state be asked if it would like to change its name?

- **A.** Relief

7. Q. What question is asked during the Removal Action?

- **A.** Do you want that person here in your space or do you want your space clear? It is up to you.

8. Q. What is Sensory Experience Memory (SEM)?

- **A.**　SEM is a feeling memory.

9. Q.　What does SEM have to do with states Vaded with Fear or Rejection?

- **A.**　When the state is Vaded with fear or rejection it is the SEM, the bad feeling memory, that comes up giving unwanted feelings. The ISE is bridged in order to change the SEM from that which is currently carried by the Vaded State.

10. Q.　How can SEM be helpful during the therapeutic process?

- **A.**　When the client is able to take on the persona of another person and then return to their own Resource State, that enables the client to gain a more full understanding. This is what happens when the client uses Introject speak to understand that a parent was not able to share unconditional love. This is also what happens when the client is able to use the changing chairs Introject action in order to better understand the dynamic in the relationship with another person.

Day 2 Crossword Answers

Across

- 3. ISE is the Initial Sensitizing ____ /Event
- 4. What you need from every Resource State you work with 1,4 /A Name
- 6. SEM is the Sensory Experience ____ /Memory
- 7. A state that does not like or understand another state /Conflicted
- 9. The number of steps in Bridging /Three
- 10. The Action that comes before Expression /Bridging
- 15. A good or bad emotional memory /SEM
- 16. Whose name is called when asking for a helping state? 3,7 /The Clients
- 17. A state is in the ____ when it picks or approves its name /Conscious

Down

- 1. Name this state with its purpose not its behavior /Retro
- 2. Bridging is used for states vaded with __ or Rejection /Fear

- 5. After Bridging, rather than change the memory, we change the ___ /Emotion
- 8. The most empowering Action for to a State Vaded with Fear /Expression
- 11. Bridging moves from the unwanted emotion to the ___ /ISE
- 12. Action when a Vaded State may get a new name /Relief
- 13. The Introject is told to stay or go in this Action /Removal
- 14. Introject Speak is used with a State Vaded with ... /Rejection
- 16. Conflicted States both want to be Conscious at the same ___ /Time

11.3 Day 3 Answers

1. **Q. What two questions are asked when using the Find Resource Action in order to locate a preferred Resource?**

- **A.** What is it that you want to experience during this time both internally and externally? What do you want to feel and how do you want to act?

2. **Q. When the client cannot remember a time that their preferred Resource was Conscious, what can the therapist do?**

- **A.** Have the client to describe either what it would be like if they had a Resource that could do what they would like to do, or have the client to describe another person who can do what they would like to do really well. In the middle of their explanation stop them, ask what can I call this part of you that is speaking right now, and then ask that Resource if it would be willing to help the client in the future with this activity because it has such a good handle on what is required.

3. **Q. What type of State ruminates?**

- **A.** States Vaded with Confusion

4. **Q. Pouting is an example of the behavior of what type of pathological state?**

- **A.** Retro Original States

5. **Q. PTSD is an example of what type of pathological state?**

- **A.** States Vaded with Fear

6. **Q. Feelings of being unworthy, or not good enough, are an example of what type of pathological state?**

- **A.** States Vaded with Rejection

7. **Q. What type of pathological state is only pathological in that it is the wrong state to be out at a certain time?**

- **A.** Dissonant States

8. **Q. What is the Imagery Check Action used for?**

- **A.** This action indicates to the client that Therapy has been useful, and it indicates to the therapist that more work on this issue may not need to be done. If the imagery check indicates no improvement then further work needs to be done.

9. **Q. How many types of pathological Resource States are there?**
- **A.** Eight
10. **Q. Gambling is an example of what type of pathological state?**
- A Retro Avoiding State

Day 3 Crossword Answers

Across

5 - I am anorexic. /Rejection/Anorexics have a need for the connection they get from feeling the care they get when they are underweight.

6 - I want to sleep, but I feel a lot of anxiety. /Fear/The experience of the anxiety means a vaded state is conscious. While this could be Confusion or Rejection, it is most normally Fear.

8 - I procrastinate. /Conflicted/One state wants to get work done and another state wants to do something else.

9 - Since my partner died I don't feel like doing anything. /Disappointment/The disappointed state is blocking all other states from enjoying anything.

10 - I withdraw when things are hard. /Original/Withdrawal is a coping skill people can develop in childhood to stay out of trouble.

14 - I am lazy and I need to get work done. /Conflicted/A rest state is in conflict with a work state.

16 - I'm afraid people will laugh at me. /Rejection/Afraid of not being good enough.

Down

1 - I want to sleep, but I just think about things instead. /Conflicted/A thinking state wants to think and a rest state wants to sleep. It is not vaded because there is no emotions.

2 - There is no part of me that wants to do anything. /Disappointed/An upset state is blocking.

3 - I get really upset when he criticises me. /Rejected/The 'rejected state' feels non-accepted.

4 - I can't get what he did out of my head. It even keeps me up at night. /Confusion/Rumination.

7 - My rage is really out of control. /Original/A tantrum state from childhood is trying to help.

11 - I work day and night and can't stop. /Avoiding/A Retro Avoiding state is helping the client not feel the anxiety of a state Vaded with Fear or Rejection.

12 - When I try to study, I just think about other things I would like to do. /Dissonant/A state is out that is not emotional and does not want to be in the situation.

13 - I have night terrors. /Fear/An unresolved state is afraid of something at the ISE.

15 - I have panic attacks. /Fear/A Vaded State with Fear is entering the Conscious.

Day 3 Activity Answers

1. When my boss criticizes me I just feel like crawling in a hole. /Rejection
2. I know it is safe, but I can't get on an elevator. /Fear
3. I shop way too much. /Avoiding
4. I think I love him, but I get scared and pull back. /Rejection
5. I am out of control with my gambling. /Avoiding
6. I have OCD. /Avoiding
7. I am not playing my sport as good as I know I can. /Dissonant
8. I am self-harming. /Avoiding
9. I keep thinking about the accident that killed her. /Confusion
10. I am afraid of the dark. /Fear
11. I have a lot of anxiety when I am in a group. /Rejection
12. Sometimes I speak well and sometimes I just want to. /Dissonant (no emotion)
13. People don't give me a chance. /Rejection
14. When I am criticised I get angry. /Avoiding (Retro state is protecting a fragile state)

11.4 Day 4 Answers

1. **Q. During resolution, is it important that a perpetrator be able to express using, Introject Speak?**

- **A.** No, unless the client has a need to understand why a perpetrator would do such a thing, there is no value in using Introject Speak to give voice to a perpetrator.

2. **Q. What is the one word that best describes how a state Vaded with Confusion exhibits?**

- **A.** Rumination

3. **Q. What is SEM?**

- **A.** Sensory experience memory, which is re-experiencing a feeling from the past. It may, or may not, be connected to an intellectual memory, i.e., a client may re-experience a bad feeling and not know where it came from.

4. **Q. How does SEM help a client gain a better understanding when using the Changing Chairs Introject Action?**

- **A.** After a client sits in the chair of another person and speaks as that person, and then returns to their own chair and they carry with them the SEM of what that Introject felt. It is this SEM that allows them to gain a higher perspective, even more than what the Introject said.

5. **Q. What type of pathological state is evident when a client is depressed?**

- **A.** A State Vaded with Disappointment

6. **Q. When should the name of the Introject be first called out, by the therapist when using the Changing Chairs Action?**

- **A.** Just as the client is in the process of setting in to the chair of the Introject.

7. **Q. Why is it better to instruct a client to change chairs, rather than ask for their permission?**

- **A.** It is the therapist who is the professional and who decides a course of Therapy. Clients should not be bothered with having to make therapeutic decisions. They might make the wrong decisions and they might have anxiety over what the right decision is.

8. **Q. What should be done if the client does not speak directly to the Introject in the empty chair?**

- **A.** The therapist can speak first to the Introject in an empty chair and then say, "Now you go ahead and tell him." It is highly important for the client to speak directly to the Introject in an empty chair. It is when the client speaks directly to the Introject that the confused Resource State comes to the surface.

9. **Q. Why is it important to call out the Introjects name, and ask the Introject how he or she feels about what has just been said?**

- **A.** By calling out the name of the Introject as the client is in the process of sitting down, and by immediately asking how what the client said makes the Introject feel, the client is better able to speak as the Introject.

10. **Q. When are states most normally Vaded with Confusion?**
   A. During adulthood

- **Activity (with answers) Day 4**

Describe in detail what occurs during each of the following steps.

1. **Vivify Specific to the Confused State.** /The state that is Confused must be Conscious before it can get the understanding it (specifically) needs.

2. **Ask what needs to be said and/or asked.** /This pinpoints exactly what the Confused State is confused about, and gives the therapist needed information to promote the right statements and questions when the state speaks directly to the Introject.

3. **Create an understanding of the Introject in the other chair.** /This prepares the client for speaking to the Introject. It also promotes the Confused State to be even more Conscious.

4. **Ensure complete expression and questions.** /By looking at the notes from point 2 above, and prompting the client, the client will express all aspects of the confusion.

5. **Direct the client to move to the Introject's chair.** the Introject should be asked how it feels /The therapist ensures that all points raised by the Confused State are responded to by the Introject.

6. **Speak directly with the Introject.** /It is important for the therapist and the client each to speak directly to the Introject during the process.

7. **Direct the client back to the original chair.** /Tell the client to stand, move over to the other chair, then as the client is sitting down, call the client by name.

8. **Debrief** /Discuss how the client feels and what the client has learned.

11.5 Day 5 Answers

1. **Q. What type of pathological Resource State causes panic disorder?**
   - **A.** A State Vaded with Fear
2. **Q. What type of pathological Resource State is associated with low self-esteem?**
   - **A.** A State Vaded with Rejection
3. **Q. When working with an ISE relating to sexual abuse, is it important that details be obtained?**
   - **A.** No, it is only important that the Vaded State becomes empowered by speaking to the Introject. No detail needs to be disclosed.
4. **Q. Why should therapists not assume that a pathological issue is necessarily related to sexual abuse?**
   - **A.** Everyone has pathological issues, and not everyone was sexually abused. It is often the case that a person who was sexually abused presents with a problem that is not related to that abuse. Bridging will help determine if their issue is related to abuse or related to something else.
5. **Q. What if bridging takes the client to an issue other than sexual abuse when their client thought their problem was because of sexual abuse?**
   - **A.** Clients come to therapy to resolve what they are ready to change. It is the role of the Resource Therapist to bring the problematic Resource State into the Conscious and help that Resource State find normality. There is no need to revisit any kind of abuse, if it is not related to the problem the client wants to change. Of course, if bridging goes to abuse then that is where the client needs to become empowered.
6. **Q. What type of pathological Resource State is associated with anorexia?**
   - **A.** A State Vaded with Rejection

7. **Q. What type of pathological Resource State is associated with bulimia?**

- **A.** A State Vaded with Rejection

8. **Q. What benefit does an anorexic client gain from losing weight?**

- **A.** A deep feeling of connection with a parent.

9. **Q. Why should the Introject of the rejecting parent be spoken with by the therapist when revisiting the ISE?**

- **A.** In order for the state Vaded with Rejection to realize that it was the parent's inability to show unconditional love, not that the child was unlovable.

10. **Q. What comment should be made to the Vaded State after speaking with the Introject of a rejecting parent?**

- **A.** "Boy, I can see why you feel the way you have felt. Anyone would feel that way. Your parent was not very good at that time in showing you the unconditional love that every child deserves. I want to make sure that you get that." Then, a nurturing state can be brought in during the Relief action.

11.6 Day 6 Answers

1. **Q. What is the difference between a Retro Original and a Retro Avoiding State?**

   - **A.** A Retro Original States learned its unwanted behavior at the time it was formed during childhood. This behavior will have been evident since childhood. A Retro Avoiding state learned its behavior to help the client avoid the bad feelings of a Vaded State. This can happen any time, but often this is learned during adulthood.

2. **Q. Is a state Vaded with Confusion, or a state Vaded with Disappointment, more closely associated with depression?**

   - **A.** A State Vaded with Disappointment

3. **Q. Why do some people have addictions?**

   - **A.** Psychological addictions are Retro Avoiding States that are helping the client avoid the negative feelings of a state Vaded with Fear or Rejection.

4. **Q. What is the difference between a physical addiction and a psychological addiction?**

   - **A.** A physiological addiction is when the body becomes accustomed to a chemical or food, while a psychological addiction is an avoidance behavior.

5. **Q. Is OCD more associated with depression or addiction?**

   - **A.** OCD is a form of addiction

6. **Q. What type of pathological state is associated with addiction?**

   - **A.** A Retro Avoiding state that is avoiding the feelings of a state Vaded with Fear or Rejection

7. **Q. Why is Retro State Negotiation used to help someone who is depressed?**

   - **A.** Retro State Negotiation is used to assist a state to find a new role. A state that is Disappointed often needs to find a new role where it can feel positive about its contribution.

8. **Q. Why is Find Resource used to help someone who is depressed?**

- **A.** It is important for someone who is depressed to start regaining physiological energy. Therefore, it is important to find two resources that have been able to enjoy activities in the past. These resources may be asked if they would be willing to reengage with their roles, if the disappointed state is able to grant them permission to do this.

9. **Q. How should the State Vaded with Disappointment be spoken with by the Therapist?**

- **A.** The State Vaded with disappointment should be spoken to by the Therapist with empathy and understanding. The Therapist should indicate that it is very understandable that the state feels upset. By showing an empathetic understanding the State Vaded with Disappointment is more likely to allow other states to begin interacting in life in a positive way.

10. **Q. What type of pathological state is associated with rage behavior?**

- **A.** Retro Original

Activity (with answers) Day 6

Describe when it is important to work with a Vaded State in order to stop Retro Behavior, and when this is not important.

When a Retro State is Retro Original there is no need to work with a Vaded State, because the Retro Original State learned its behavior in childhood as a coping skill, and it is not avoiding behavior that is associated to a Vaded State.

When a Retro State is Retro Avoiding it is important to resolve the Vaded State before Retro State Negotiation, otherwise the Retro State will want to continue the Retro Behavior.

Why is it important to do Retro State Negotiation after resolving the associated Vaded State when working with a client who has Retro Avoiding behavior?

> If the Retro Avoiding State does not find a positive way it can be helpful, in the future when the client is stressed that state can re-engage with its old behavior to help the client deal with the stress. If a preferred behavior is agreed to using Retro State Negotiation, then the old, unwanted, behavior will not be used again.

11.7 Day 7 Answers

Quiz (with answers) Day 7

1. **Q. When should client confidentiality be breached?**
- **A.** When the client or another person is in danger.
2. **Q. What are two benefits of Resource Mapping?**
- **A.** Resource Mapping helps clients understand what resources they have available, and Resource Mapping helps identify Resource States that may need further therapeutic assistance.
3. **Q. How is Resource Mapping used in the relationship counseling?**
- **A.** Each partner receives a Resource Mapping session where Resource States that are involved in the disagreement are mapped, where an intellectual state that can hear criticism is mapped, and where Resource States that enjoy the relationship are mapped. These states are used to helping clients achieve better communication and a more positive relationship.
4. **Q. How often are questions asked during active listening?**
- **A.** Never
5. **Q. How often are suggestions given during active listening?**
- **A.** Never
6. **Q. What is the value of active listening?**
- **A.** Active listening allows a client or a Resource State to feel heard and allows a client or Resource State to more easily describe their feelings.
7. **Q. Why is it appropriate to charge more for a Resource Mapping session?**
- **A.** The therapist must type out the Resource map in order to give it to the client. This takes time.
8. **Q. What should the therapist do when during a Resource Mapping session a state appears with a psychological issue?**

- **A.** The therapist should ask the client if the client wants to go ahead and resolve the psychological issue. Clients normally prefer to resolve issues that come up.

9. **Q. What do we mean by dual relationships when talking about ethics in therapy?**

- **A.** A dual relationship is when a therapist has another type of relationship with a client, for example a friendship, or a work relationship. Generally, these relationships should be avoided so clients are more able to be self-revealing to a person who they will not encounter elsewhere in life.

10. **Q. Is it likely that all states will be mapped during a Resource Mapping session?**

- **A.** No

11.8 Day 8 Answers

1. **Q. Is a pain that is situationally based more likely to be organic or psychosomatic?**
   - **A.** Psychosomatic
2. **Q. Is PTSD more likely to be organic or psychosomatic?**
   - **A.** Psychosomatic
3. **Q. Is ADHD more likely to be organic or psychosomatic?**
   - **A.** Organic
4. **Q. Is panic disorder more likely to be organic or psychosomatic?**
   - **A.** Psychosomatic
5. **Q. Is psychosis more likely to be organic or psychosomatic?**
   - **A.** Organic
6. **Q. Is manic-depression more likely to be organic or psychosomatic?**
   - **A.** Organic
7. **Q. Is anorexia more likely to be organic or psychosomatic?**
   - **A.** Psychosomatic
8. **Q. Why is it not advisable to suggest to a client that a pain will not be felt?**
   - **A.** An underlying Resource State may take on this pain and cause the client psychological or physiological problems.
9. **Q. How can an underlying state be used to help a client control organic pain?**
   - **A.** An underlying Resource State that is brave and wants to be useful may be asked to take on the sensations of an organic pain so that Surface States do not have to feel them in their full intensity.
10. **Q. How do you help someone if the pain is considered to be psychosomatic?**

- **A.** It is important to find the Resource State that is causing the pain and make sure that it returns to normality so it will no longer have a need to cause a negative sensation.

11.9 Day 9 Answers

Quiz (with answers) Day 9

1. **Q. What is an Introject?**
- **A.** An Introject is an internal impression of a person, an animal, or an inanimate.

2. **Q. What is a Resource State?**
- **A.** A Resource State is a part of the personality that was formed through repetitious behavior during childhood. It is a physiological part of the brain formed by the growth of axons and dendrite and trained synaptic firings.

3. **Q. What is an OPI?**
- **A.** Another Personalized Introject is a state that reports not being part of the client, and not really belonging where it is. It appears that this state and the client can both benefit from it going to where it belongs.

4. **Q. What is a CFI?**
- **A.** A creative form identity is a Resource State that expresses itself in a creative way such as a wall, a hand, or even an animal.

5. **Q. Why is it important to present the use of the Separation Sieve as, just an experiment?**
- **A.** The Separation Sieve is often used when there is a reluctance to let something go. By introducing the use of the separation sieve as merely an experiment, it can be viewed as safe by the state that is reluctant to let something go. Following the separation, the state can be asked what it prefers.

6. **Q. How can the Separation Sieve be used to reduce guilt?**
- **A.** Guilt is a heavy, blaming, emotion. The state holding the guilt can be instructed to temporarily slide through the sieve, just as an experiment, to see what it would be like to be separate from the guilt, from the heavy emotion that the sieve cannot allow through.

7. **Q. How can the Separation Sieve be used as an alternative to Bridging and Vaded State resolution?**

- **A.** The separation sieve can be used as a secondary alternative to Bridging and Vaded State resolution. The Vaded State can be instructed to come through the sieve, temporarily leaving all of its heaviness, fear, and sense of rejection in the sieve. Then it can be asked if it wants any of that back, and if not, whatever has been caught within the sieve can be sizzled away. The separation sieve is a metaphor that allows experimentation and a more clear understanding about what is preferred.

8. **Q. What is the state sometimes referred to as Inner Self?**
- **A.** The Inner Self state refers to itself as always having been present, even at birth. It always speaks with a strong, clear voice. And it seems to have an understanding about what is best for the client. It sometimes refers to itself as higher self, or other such names.

9. **Q. How can Inner Self sometimes be used in Therapy?**
- **A.** The Inner Self state can be used to help a client gain perspective on what is wanted or important in life.

10. **Q. How does a client normally report feeling following an OPI leaving?**
- **A.** The client almost always reports feeling lighter.

Activity (with answers) Day 9

Fill in the following table with either, Resource, Introject, Inner Self, CFI, or OPI

1.	It is the one state that everyone appears to have.	Inner Self
2.	It is a physiological part of the brain.	Resource
3.	When we bridge we always go to one of them.	Resource
4.	They report that they are not part of the person.	OPI
5.	It speaks with a clear, strong, caring voice.	Inner Self
6.	They report that they are not where they should be.	OPI

7.	We can feel an inner peace when they respect each other and get along.	Resource
8.	They are created by a Resource State when it takes on an internalized impression.	Introject
9.	They are created by repetition usually in childhood.	Resource
10.	It claims to have wisdom about the purpose of the person.	Inner Self
11.	They are Resource States and are like Resource States in all ways other than their self-identification.	CFI
12.	They identify themselves as a part of the body or as some other creative form.	CFI
13.	They can leave and afterward Resource States continue to report that they are no longer present.	OPI
14.	A Vaded Resource State is vaded because of the impressions it holds about these.	Introject
15.	They cannot be destroyed and they cannot leave.	Resource
16.	They can slightly change their role, and they can change the amount they come out.	Resource

11.10 Day 10 Answers

1. **Q. What type of pathological state is most likely involved in writers block?**

- **A.** A Dissonant State

2. **Q. What type of pathological state is most likely involved in a sporting slump?**

- **A.** A Dissonant State

3. **Q. How do you tell the difference between a Dissonant State and a Vaded State?**

- **A.** The Vaded State feels emotionally out of control, while the Dissonant State feels uncomfortable and wishes it was not out.

4. **Q. If a client reports being highly emotional when attempting to talk in front of a group what type of pathological state is likely involved?**

- **A.** A Vaded State

5. **Q. If a client reports being uncomfortable and unable to think clearly when attempting to talk in front of a group what type of pathological state is likely involved?**

- **A.** A Dissonant State

6. **Q. What is the name of the international Resource Therapy organization?**

- **A.** Resource Therapy International

7. **Q. Who gets to have a name listed in the International Resource Therapy organization database, as a qualified clinical Resource Therapist?**

- **A.** Therapists who have finished the clinical qualification training, and who see themselves as a Resource Therapist, and who are actively practicing Resource Therapy may be listed on the Resource Therapy International website. The listing is to assist clients and therapists to be able to find qualified Clinical Resource Therapists.

8. **Q. What is a therapeutic anchor?**

- **A.** A therapeutic anchor is, for example, an animal Association with the Resource State that can be used to bring that Resource State into the Conscious whenever that Resource State is preferred.

9. **Q. Why is it important to vivify the client as an animal in order to bring out a preferred Resource State?**

- **A.** When a client chooses the animal that is most closely associated with the Resource State, and the client is able to feel what that animal feels like, imagining being that animal can assist the client in bringing out the associated Resource State.

10. **Q. What is the best animal for a client to select?**

- **A.** It does not matter. The client can choose any animal and may even choose something other than an animal as an anchor as long as it is chosen by the client as the preferred imagery for that Resource State to associate itself with.

Day 3 Crossword Answers

Across

- 1. An unwanted behavior learned in childhood is Retro /Original
- 4. A state is a healthy condition is ___ /Normal
- 7. Most Fear and Rejection Vaded states were vaded in ___. /Childhood
- 12. A person with depression has a state Vaded with /Disappointment
- 13. When a state is Vaded with Fear or Rejection we use __ to get to ISE. /Bridging
- 15. When a less preferred state is Conscious there is a ___ state./Dissonant
- 17. A state that often comes into the Conscious is a __ State. /Surface
- 18. What is switched during the Changing Chairs Action? /Chairs

Down

- 2. When most states are Vaded with Confusion. /Adulthood
- 3. A person with PTSD has a state Vaded with ___. /Fear
- 5. A behavior that keeps a person from feeling bad /Avoiding

- 6. A state that rarely comes into the Conscious is an ___ State. /Underlying
- 8. When a state is out it is ___. /Conscious
- 9. A technique to help the client learn to bring out a state. /Anchoring
- 10. A person consumed with guilt has a state Vaded with /Confusion
- 11. A person who is over competitive has a state Vaded with ___. /Rejection
- 14. Bridging takes us to the ___. /ISE
- 16. To bring a state out we Vivify ___. /Specific

12 Appendix 2 Core Concepts by Day

Core Concepts for Day 1 Training

Topic	Page	Notes
Goals	21	
Resource States	22	
Conscious	23	
Introjects	23	
Surface States	25	
Underlying States	25	
History	26	
Alters	28	
Nature of States	29	
Formation	30	
Normal States	32	
Vaded	32	
Retro	35	
Dissonant	37	
Conflicted	37	

Core Concepts for Day 1 Training

Actions	37	
Vivify Specific Action 2	38	
Bridging Action 3	39	

Core Concepts for Day 2 Training

Topic	Page	Notes
Naming States	49	
Action 4 Expression	51	
Action 5 Introject Speak	52	
Action 6 Removal	54	
Action 7 Relief	54	
Finding a helping State	56	
Conflicted State Negotiation	65	
Imagery Check	61	
Sensory Experience Memory	62	

Core Concepts for Day 3 Training

Topic	Page	Notes
Diagnosis: Action 1	73	
Vaded with Fear	78	
Vaded with Rejection	80	
Vaded with Confusion	82	
Vaded with Disappointment	83	
Retro Original	84	
Retro Avoiding	85	
Conflicted	88	
Dissonant	90	
Difference between a Dis-sonant State and a Retro State	91	

Core Concepts for Day 4 Training

Topic	Page	Notes
Vaded with Confusion vs Vaded with Disappointment	98	

Working with a State Vaded with Confusion	99	
The Changing Chairs Introject Action	99	
Importance of Sensory Experience Memory in this Action	101	
Loss and Grief	102	
Heavy Emotions	104	

Core Concepts for Day 5 Training

Topic	Page	Notes
Panic Disorder	110	
Anorexia and Bulimia	112	
Sexual and other Abuse	115	
Working with a State Vaded with Fear	117	
Working with a State Vaded with Rejection	120	

Core Concepts for Day 6 Training

Topic	Page	Notes
Diagnosis: Action 1	128	

Difference in Retro Original and Retro Avoiding	130	
Addictions	132	
Anger/Rage issues	136	
Working with Depression	139	
Keeping purpose and trading purviews	144	
Retro State Negotiation: Action 10	130	

Core Concepts for Day 7 Training

Topic	Page	Notes
Ethics Confidentiality	148	
Ethic Duel Relationships	149	
Active Listening	150	
Resource Mapping	150	
Role	152	
Name	152	
Knowledge and impressions of other states	153	
What it can offer in the future	154	

RT Couples Counselling	159	

Core Concepts for Day 8 Training

Topic	Page	Notes
Pain and Somatic Symptoms	164	
Organic Symptoms	165	
Psychosomatic Symptoms	165	
How to tell?	165	
Organic Intervention	167	
Psychosomatic Intervention	168	
Action 13: Resistance Alliancing	169	
Acknowledgement, Appreciation and Suggestion	169	
Engagement Method	170	

Core Concepts for Day 9 Training

Topic	Page	Notes

What lies within? Resource State	176	
Inner Self	181	
Introject	178	
OPI	185	
CFI	182	
Using the Separation Sieve	188	

Core Concepts for Day 10 Training

Topic	Page	Notes
Vaded with Fear	199	
Vaded with Rejection	199	
Vaded with Confusion	199	
Vaded with Disappointment	200	
Retro Original	200	
Retro Avoiding	200	
Conflicted	201	
Working with Dissonant parts	201	
Action 15 Anchoring	201	

Common Supervision Issues	203	

13 Glossary

Changing Chairs Introject Action: This is a resource activity designed to assist clients to hold less confusion in relation to an Introject. The client is instructed to imagine the essence of an Introject in an empty chair, to say everything that they would like to say to that Introject, then to move into that chair and speak as the Introject back to the client, expressing how what was just said made the Introject feel. It often results in a cathartic sense of understanding.

Conscious: The Conscious is held by the Resource State that is currently aware and behaving. When a different Resource State takes over the Conscious, sense of self, emotions, behavior and abilities, change. The Conscious awareness may change from intellectual and reflective to reactive and emotional with a change of Resource State.

Conflicted States: Resources in a conflicted condition are in a level of conflict with another Resource to the extent that the individual experiences psychological distress. While it is common and appropriate that Resources hold different opinions (I would really like the car, and there's no way I can afford a new car) Conflicted States achieve a level of conflict that becomes stressful to the client.

Dissonant State: A Resource State that is in the Conscious at the wrong time.

Resource (State): A personality part that was created by the repetition of returning over and over again to a coping skill. It is a physiological part of the nervous system created by axon and dendrite growth and trained synaptic firings. Each Resource manifests the traits of the coping skills that formed it. Each will have its own level of emotion, intellect, and abilities. Whenever a person is Conscious there is a Resource holding the Conscious.

Resource Personality Theory: A theory that assumes that personality is composed of separate parts, called Resources. Resource therapists assume that the most direct way to promote change is to work specifically with the Resource that is troubled, rather than with an intellectual state that can easily talk about the problem.

Imagery Check: At the beginning of the intervention the Vivify Specific Action is used to locate the Resource that requires change. Following the intervention, the Imagery Check is used to return to this initial image to test the effectiveness of the intervention, to give the client practice in a similar setting in the future, and to give the client confidence that the intervention has been effective. If the Imagery Check reveals no change, there is an indication that more therapeutic work is required relating to the issue.

Intellectual Memory: An Intellectual Memory is one that when recalling an occurrence the emotional experience is not relived. Intellectual memories may be held by states that did not experience the original event. Sensory Experience Memories differ from Intellectual memories in that the recalling process includes the emotional experience of the original event.

Intellectual Protector States: These are protector states that come to the Conscious to protect the personality from the emotional feelings of Vaded States. During therapy Intellectual Protector States may attempt to block the therapist from Bridging to the Vaded State that needs resolution. The client intellectualizes, rather than feels. The Intellectual Protector State normally dislikes the Vaded State, seeing it as a state that gets in the way.

Initial Sensitising Event: This is a difficult and emotional event that has overwhelmed a Normal Resource, causing it to become a Vaded State. Later, when this Vaded State comes to the Conscious it brings with it the same negative emotional feelings that it experienced during the initial sensitizing event.

Introject: A Resource's internalized impression of another person, an animal, or an inanimate. Most Introjects are experienced as emotionally positive, but Vaded States hold Introjects from which they have experienced negative emotion. Introjects have only the power given them by the Resource States that hold them.

Normal States: Resources in the Normal condition exhibit psychological health. They function well both externally and within the personality. They are not conflicted with other states and they do not hold psychological distress.

Protector States: Therapeutic resistance is caused by protector states. These are states that attempt to protect fragile Vaded States from coming to the Conscious where the personality would experience the overwhelming emotions they feel. Behavioral examples of protector states coming into the Conscious include anger, withdrawal, intellectualizing, and perseveration. Protector States merely deflect attention, while Retro Avoiding States conduct unwanted behavior to save the personality from the negative feelings of Vaded States.

Retro Avoiding States: Retro States that learn to hold the Conscious to avoid the experience of a Vaded State. In problem gambling, the state that gambles is a Retro Avoiding State. It has learned to protect the client from a painful Vaded emotion filled state by filling the Consciousness with gambling activity. Other Resources will dislike this gambling Resource, but the Retro State believes its role in saving the client from the negative emotions of the Vaded State is more important than the disapproval it endures. Other examples of Retro Avoiding States include the states that cause a client to feel numb, states that act out OCD behavior, self-harming states, and states that are involved with eating disorder activities. These states will hold a strong compulsion to maintain their helping behavior as long as the emotional state they protect the client from remains vaded.

Retro Original States: These are states that have learned a functional coping skill in childhood that is no longer wanted by the client. Much antisocial behavior is a result of Retro Original States and examples include passive aggressive behavior and rage. These Retro States will continue to see their role as important, until they can be negotiated with to take on an altered or lesser role.

Retro States: Resources that, when conscious, act in ways that other Resources (and usually other people) find problematic. There are two types of Retro States, Retro Original States and Retro Avoiding States. Antisocial behavior, gambling, OCD behavior, and Eating Disorder behavior are examples of Retro States assuming the Conscious.

Sensory Experience Memory: A Sensory Experience Memory is one that, when experienced, the person emotionally re-experiences the original event. A Sensory Experience Memory is most normally experienced only closer in time to the event. For example, immediately after experiencing something emotional, good or bad, it is common to relive the emotional experience during recall. As time passes, most Sensory Experience Memories are transformed into Intellectual Memories. Sensory Experience Memories may only be experienced in the longer term when the Resource State that had the original experience is holding the Conscious.

States Vaded with Confusion: Following an initial sensitizing event, this Resource is left with a fundamental and profound level of confusion, and its response to this lack of ability to understand is a profoundly uncomfortable unknowing. While Resources Vaded with Fear, Rejection, or Disappointment hold a distinctly negative emotion, Resources Vaded with Confusion exhibit anxiety about what is not known to a level that is problematic to the client. These states are often characterised by rumination.

States Vaded with Disappointment: This Resource takes on an overwhelming feeling of disappointment because of the gulf between what was desired or expected in life and the perceived reality. It is not the magnitude of what has happened that vades this Resource, it is the interpretation of what has happened that vades the state. These states cause psychological depression.

States Vaded with Fear: Resources Vaded with Fear are carrying internal fear everywhere they go and when they come to the Conscious they bring it to the surface with them. Resources Vaded with Fear prevent clients from feeling free to live their lives in a way that they choose, and they are the root of many psychological disturbances.

States Vaded with Rejection: Resources Vaded with Rejection feel unlovable. This feeling of not being good enough drives the client, when it comes to the Conscious, to experience emotions of disempowerment, and they sometimes create a need to be perfect, as expressed in over competitiveness, out-of-control purchasing, and eating disorders.

Surface Resources: Surface Resources, as opposed to Underlying Resources, are those that are used frequently. They normally share memories together, and often observe other surface states when one is in the Conscious. A Resource that is out at work, and a Resource that is out while travelling are examples of Surface States.

Underlying Resources: Underlying Resources, as opposed to Surface Resources, are those that have been out frequently in the past but currently seldom come into the Conscious. Most childhood states are underlying Resources, with memories not readily available to surface states. Vaded States are most commonly underlying states, which occasionally come to the Conscious harbouring feelings of angst.

Vaded Avoided States: Vaded States are problematic for a client in two ways, they can be Vaded Conscious States or Vaded Avoided States. Vaded Avoided States do not hold the Conscious, but when they come near or temporarily into the Conscious a 'helping state' (a Retro Avoiding State) uses an addictive behavior to force the Vaded State out of the Conscious, saving the client from having to re-experience the overwhelmingly bad feelings of the Vaded State.

Vaded Conscious States: Vaded States are problematic for a client in two ways; they can be Vaded Conscious States or Vaded Avoided States. Vaded Conscious States come into and hold the Conscious, causing the client to feel emotional and out-of-control while they do. When they come to the surface they bring with them their overwhelming negative emotions, and this is what the client experiences when they are in the Conscious.

Vaded States: Resources that were in a Normal Condition prior to experiencing an initial sensitising event that, because there was no form of crisis intervention, left them feeling chronically overwhelmed with the negative emotions. These Resources, while in a Vaded condition, are the cause of much pathology.

Vivify Specific: This refers to vivifying a specific instance when a Resource has been in the Conscious in order to bring it back into the Conscious during therapy for the purpose of intervention. Some clients attempt to give the therapist general times a Resource has been out, and this presentation will not bring the desired Resource into the Conscious. The Vivify Specific Action requires very specific detail relating to a time the state has been conscious. During this process present tense language is used.

14 Bibliography

Blakemore, C., and Price, D. J. (1987), The organization and post-natal development of area 18 of the cat's visual cortex, Journal of Physiology, 384, pp. 293–309.

Boswell, Louis K. (1987). The initial sensitizing event of emotional disorders. Medical Hypnoanalysis Journal, 2(4), Dec, pp. 155-160.

Brewin, C. R., & Saunders, J. (2001). The effect of dissociation at encoding on intrusive memories for a stressful film. British Journal of Medical Psychology, 74, 467–472.

Bryck, Richard L.; Fisher, Philip A. (2011). Training the brain: Practical applications of neural plasticity from the intersection of cognitive neuroscience, developmental psychology, and prevention science. American Psychologist, Jul 25.

Buisseret, Pierre, Gary-Bobo, Elyane, and Imbert, Michel (1982). Plasticity in the kitten's visual cortex: Effects of the suppression of visual experience upon the orientational properties of visual cortical cells, Developmental Brain Research, 4 (4), pp. 417–26.

Davies, M. I., & Clark, D. M. (1998). Predictors of analogue posttraumatic intrusive cognitions. Behavioural and Cognitive Psychotherapy, 26, 303–314.

Emmerson, G. J. (1999). What lies within: Ego states and other internal personifications. Australian Journal of Clinical Hypnotherapy & Hypnosis, 20(1), pp. 13-22.

Emmerson, G. J. (2003, 2007, 2010). Ego state therapy. Carmarthen, Wales: Crown House Publishing

Emmerson, G. J. (2006). Advanced skills and interventions in therapeutic counseling. Carmarthen, Wales: Crown House Publishing

Emmerson, G. J. (2012). Healthy Parts Happy Self. Charleston, SC, CreateSpace.

Emmerson, G. J. (2011). Ego state personality theory. Australian Journal of Clinical Hypnotherapy and Hypnosis, 33(2), pp. 5-23.

Emmerson, G. J. (2013). Ego State Conditions. Australian Journal of Clinical Hypnotherapy and Hypnosis, 35(1), 2013. pp. 5-27.

Emmerson, G. J. (2014). Resource Therapy Primer. Blackwood Victoria, Australia: Old Golden Point Press.

Emmerson, G. J. (2014). Resource Therapy. Blackwood Victoria, Australia: Old Golden Point Press.

Emmerson, G. J. (2014). Resource Therapy Trainers Manual. Blackwood Victoria, Australia: Old Golden Point Press.

Explorable.com (Aug 27, 2011). Sensory Memory. Retrieved Feb 26, 2015 from Explorable.com: https://explorable.com/sensory-memory

Federn, P. (1953). Ego psychology and the psychosis. London: Image Publishers.

Guntrip, H. (1961). Personality structure and human interaction. London: Hogarth.

Halligan, S. L., Clark, D. M., & Ehlers, A. (2002). Cognitive processing, memory, and the development of PTSD symptoms: two experimental analogue studies. Journal of Behaviour Therapy and Experimental Psychiatry, 33, 73–89.

Holmes, E. A., Brewin, C. R., & Hennessy, R. G. (2004). Trauma films, information processing, and intrusive memory development. Journal of Experimental Psychology: General, 133(1), 3–22.

Holopainen, Debbi; Emmerson, Gordon J. (2002). Ego state therapy and the treatment of depression. Australian Journal of Clinical Hypnotherapy & Hypnosis, Vol 23(2), pp. 89-99.

Jacobson, E. (1964). The self and the object world. New York: International University Press.

Kernberg, O. (1976). Object relations theory and clinical psychoanalysis. New York: Jasonc Aronson.

Levin, Berry. (2010). Interaction of perinatal and pre-pubertal factors with genetic predisposition in the development of neural pathways involved in the regulation of energy homeostasis. Brain Research, Sep2010, Vol. 1350, p. 10-17

Muir, Darwin W., Dalhousie, U., and Mitchell, Donald E. (1973), Visual resolution and experience: Acuity deficits in cats following early selective visual deprivation, Science. 180 (4084), pp. 420–2.

Ritzman, Thomas A., (1992). Importance of identifying the initial sensitizing event. Medical Hypnoanalysis Journal, 7(3), Sep. pp. 98-104.

Schlagman, S., Kvavilashvili, L., & Schulz, J. (2007). Effects of age on involuntary autobiographical memories. In J. Mace (Ed.), Involuntary memory (pp. 87–112). Malden, MA: Blackwells.

Schrott, L. M. (1997), Effect of training and environment on brain morphology and behavior, Acta Paediatrica, 422, pp. 45–7.

Staugaard, Søren R., (2014). Involuntary memories of emotional scenes: The effects of cue discriminability and emotion over time. Journal of Experimental Psychology: General, Vol 143(5), pp. 1939-1957.

Wark, Robert C., and Peck, Carol K. (1982), Behavioral consequences of early visual exposure to contours of a single orientation, Developmental Brain Research, 5 (2), pp. 218–21.

Watkins, J. G. (1978). The therapeutic self. New York: Human Sciences.

Watkins, J. G., & Watkins, H. H. (1990). Dissociation and displacement: Where goes the "ouch?", American Journal of Clinical Hypnosis, 33, 1-10.

Watkins, J. G. & Watkins, H. H. (1997). Ego states: Theory and therapy. New York: W. W. Norton& Co.

Wilkinson, Frances, and McGill, U. (1995). Orientation, density and size as cues to texture segmentation in kittens, Vision Research, 35 (17), pp. 2463–78.

Winnicott, D. W. (1965). The maturational process and the facilitation environment. New York: International Universities Press.

Weiss, E. (1950). Principles of psychodynamics. New York: Grune & Stratton.

Index

A

Abuse 110, 115, 246
Acknowledgement, Appreciation and
    Suggestion 169
Action 1 Diagnosis 71
Action 10 Retro State Negotiation 128
Action 11 Conflicted State Negotiation 50
Action 12 Imagery Check 50
Action 13 Resistance Alliancing 164
Action 14 The Separation Sieve 176
Action 15 Anchoring 201
Action 2 Vivify Specific 21
Action 3 Bridging 21, 39
Action 4 Expression 49
Action 5 Introject Speak 49
Action 6 Removal 50
Action 7 Relief 50
Action 8 Find Resource 50
Action 9 The Changing Chairs Introject Action
    .... 98, 105
Active Listening 148, 150, 247
Addictions 132
Alters 20, 28, 243
Anger 35, 36, 77, 86, 128, 136, 247
Anorexia 76, 81, 110, 112, 113, 114, 115, 246

B

Bridging 42
Bulimia 76, 81, 110, 112, 113, 114, 115, 246

C

CFI 182
Common Supervision Issues 198, 250
Confidentiality 147, 148, 247
Conflicted States 37, 88
Conscious 23
Couples Counselling 159

Creative Form Identity 182
Crossword 47, 68, 94, 211

D

Depression 139
Dissonant 37
Dissonant States 90
Duel Relationships 147, 149, 247

E

Engagement Method 164, 170, 248

F

Feelings of low self-worth 63
Finding a helping State 50, 56, 244
Formation 20, 30, 243

G

Gambling 76, 79, 93, 222
Goals 243

H

Heavy Emotions 98, 104, 246
History 20, 26, 243

I

Inner Self 181, 194, 237, 249
Internal Conflict .... vii, 45, 73
Introjects 23

L

Loss and Grief.................................... 98, 102, 246

N

Naming States 49, 51, 244
Nature of States 20, 29, 243
Normal condition.. 20, 32
Normal States.. *32*

O

OPI..*185*
Organic Intervention 164, 248
Organic Symptoms......................... 163, 165, 248
Other Personalized Introject...........................*185*

P

Pain.............................163, 164, 165, 167, 171, 248
Panic Attacks... 63
Panic Disorder 109, 110, 246
Poor Performance .... vii, 45
protector states..157
Psychosomatic Intervention............ 164, 168, 248
Psychosomatic Symptoms 163, 165, 167, 248

Q

Quiz44, 66, 92, 106, 125, 145, 161, 172, 194, 209

R

Rage...137
Resource Mapping..150

Resource States 22
Retro Avoiding..85
Retro Original..84
Retro States..35
RT Actions..*37*

S

SEM 62
Sensory Experience Memory 62
Separation Sieve 193
Somatic Symptoms.......................... 163, 164, 248
Surface States................................20, 25, 158, 243

T

The Changing Chairs Introject Action 97, 99, 246

U

Underlying States.. 25

V

Vaded..*32*
Vaded Avoided 34
Vaded Conscious.. 34
Vaded with Confusion....................................82
Vaded with Disappointment..................... 83, 141
Vaded with Fear..78
Vaded with Rejection.. 80

W

What lies within?..176

About the author

Dr Gordon Emmerson is an Honorary Fellow in the School of Psychology at Victoria University, Melbourne. He is the author of the books 'Ego State Therapy' (2003, 2007, 2010), 'Advanced Techniques in Therapeutic Counseling (2006), Healthy Parts Happy Self (2012), Resource Therapy Primer (2014), Resource Therapy (2014), and Resource Therapy Trainer's Manual (2014). He developed Resource Personality Theory and Therapy and has developed techniques for working with many psychological conditions. As a registered psychologist and member of the Australian Psychological Society, he has published numerous refereed articles and has conducted and published experimental clinical research. Dr Emmerson has conducted workshops in Australia, South Africa, Germany, the UK, New Zealand, the US, and the Middle East. He makes keynote conference and convention addresses on his therapeutic approaches. He provides Foundation Training, a Clinical Qualification in Resource Therapy, Advanced Clinical Training in Resource Therapy, and Train the Trainer.

His and other's upcoming RT workshops can be found at the URL, http://www.resourcetherapy.com.

Gordon Emmerson, 2015